DATE DUE			
Oct. 6 '77			
OCT 1 '77			
Mar 11 78			
May 24, 79			
Dec 15 '79			

MUSIC AT YOUR
FINGERTIPS

Da Capo Press Music Reprint Series

MUSIC AT YOUR FINGERTIPS

ASPECTS OF PIANOFORTE TECHNIQUE
ADVICE FOR THE ARTIST AND AMATEUR
ON PLAYING THE PIANO

by

Ruth Slenczynska

WITH THE COLLABORATION OF
Ann M. Lingg

DA CAPO PRESS • NEW YORK • 1974

Library of Congress Cataloging in Publication Data

Slenczynska, Ruth, 1925-
  Music at your fingertips; aspects of pianoforte
technique.
    (Da Capo Press music reprint series)
    Expanded, rev. reprint of the 1968 ed. published by
Cornerstone Library, New York.
    Includes bibliographies.
    1. Piano—Practicing. I. Title.
MT220.S63 1974   786.3'04'1   74-1018
ISBN 0-306-70653-9

This Da Capo Press edition of *Music at Your Fingertips* is an
unabridged republication with corrections of the revised and ex-
panded edition published in 1968 by Cornerstone Library Publications. It is reprinted by arrangement with Doubleday and
Company, Inc.

Published by Da Capo Press, Inc.
A Subsidiary of Plenum Publishing Corporation
227 West 17th Street, New York, N.Y. 10011

MUSIC AT YOUR FINGERTIPS

MUSIC AT YOUR FINGERTIPS

ASPECTS OF PIANOFORTE TECHNIQUE

by

Ruth Slenczynska

WITH THE COLLABORATION OF

Ann M. Lingg

CORNERSTONE LIBRARY • NEW YORK

786.3041
SL 2m
9 5195
nov. 1975

CORNERSTONE LIBRARY PUBLICATIONS

are distributed by
Simon & Schuster, Inc.
630 Fifth Avenue
New York, New York 10020

Manufactured in the United States of America
under the supervision of
Rolls Offset Printing Co., Inc., N. Y.

To Catherine Vickers
Adrian Lee and
Their generation of pianists

CONTENTS

MUSIC AT YOUR FINGERTIPS

Ann M. Lingg earned her Ph.D. in musicology at the University of Vienna, and since then has written numerous books and articles on music. Her works include biographies of Mozart, Liszt, and John Philip Sousa. In addition to articles for *Reader's Digest, McCall's, Pageant,* etc., Mrs. Lingg is a regular contributor to *Opera News* which is published by the Metropolitan Opera Guild. A book entitled THE DANUBE ("the biography of a river") was written in collaboration with her late husband, Erwin Lessner.

PREFACE

WHATEVER WE know and believe, we have learned through the perception of our senses, psychologists tell us. The intensity of each sense varies with the individual. Some of us are dominated by sight perception; others receive their strongest impressions through the ear or by kinesthetic absorption. Modern education tends to dull the subtle variety of sensory reaction that exists in every child. Perhaps it is the early application of undulled sensory perception to outside stimuli that creates a child prodigy; later education can either "educate away" the child's untutored acuteness of reaction or stimulate certain traits that will develop into artistic individuality. Many of the recommendations on practice methods given here may seem general and over-simple; yet they are the result of thirty years experience, applied during years of teaching at every level, and again polished and broadened for a revived and extremely active concert career. I am not repeating to you, like a parrot, the many little things about specific problems that my own teachers taught me, but rather the principles behind them. I have kept perfecting the foundation that was mine at fourteen, in years of experience, until I have acquired a set of tools that may be useful to others who pursue the same pianistic goal.

First and foremost, I was taught to listen (as distinguished from "hearing") and to learn from all sources with an open, credulous, and investigating mind and with the determination to make a piece "sound right," regardless of the means required to achieve this end.

In 1929, when I was four, I had some lessons with a Leschetizky pupil, Mrs. Alma Schmidt-Kennedy. After every lesson, she delighted me with a story from Greek mythology. This opened to me the world of images and imagination, made me understand the connection between imagery and music, and implanted in me the idea that a good musician is interested in many different things for their own sake.

In 1929 I also met Josef Hofmann, of the Curtis Institute, and a year later I had a few lessons with him. Five years after that we happened to cross the Atlantic on the same boat. During our week aboard the S.S. *Washington* he spent practically all his free time with me and instilled in me the idea that even technical problems are controlled by the mind. I came to realize that sufficient mental effort produces a satisfactory solution, whatever the difficulty.

In 1930-31 I worked under Egon Petri, who combined a disconcerting contradiction of magnificent technical ability with excessive modesty in his speech. He taught me many important technical expediencies. He thought in terms of "I'll try my very best and hope it will come out well", which is dangerous for a youngster because often the very best he can do doesn't come out well at all. I became unhappy to the point of self-despisement and didn't regain confidence until 1934, when I had Rachmaninoff to guide me. "Who are you?" he would say. "You're only a child. Why should your best be good enough? Don't look into a mirror; look at the music!"

In 1931-32 I studied Beethoven, Bach, Schubert, and Mozart with Artur Schnabel, who gave me freedom and assuredness through his inflexible, literal interpretation. Every one of his performances followed an unchanging master plan, even though he was free within his own boundaries. No other pianist, then or now, thought quite in this manner—perhaps a lost art.

Alfred Cortot, with whom I worked from 1932 for seven years, was just the opposite. He taught me to improvise. "Music is poetry. Once you have played, it's over. You can never express the same thing twice in the same way."

I had many other teachers, some of them less famous. My father supervised my studies from infancy. For three years I took lessons from Marguerite Long, who made me supersensitive to the timbre of every note. For two seasons I worked with Lazare Lévy, a genius for inventive fingering.

Isidor Philipp gave me books of his finger exercises, and those of Brahms. Nadia Boulanger taught me harmony, mainly by making me analyze Bach's chorales. My family and I lived in Europe most of the time; in 1939, after the war forced us to return home for good, Dr. Albert Elkus, then head of the Music Department of the University of California, kindled my interest in books on music; I began to study the lives of the great composers and to explore the music libraries, which I still do.

In this book I am not meting out musical advice; rather I discuss practice method. For the student the main psychological advantage of taking lessons is the stimulus from an outside source he respects, until such time as he can find the stimulus within himself. Every great artist once started as a student who gradually assimilated his own concepts, tested methods and musical thoughts, learned from false start and failure as well as from success, developed his musical personality through knowledge, hard work, and optimism. The most celebrated virtuoso and the most inexperienced student work with the same raw material, the printed score, the only true authority. All the teacher can do is to give the budding musician a reliable set of tools and to spark the love for music and the desire to communicate.

PERSONAL FACTORS

WHAT MAKES a composition a work of art? What is the special quality that starts a chain of inspirations that stay with the listener and stimulate creative thought of his own? A Beethoven symphony has remained popular through one and a half centuries, fresh through thousands of performances, because its creative fire continues to kindle the imagination, to stir emotion in all of us. It is impossible to miss the spirit of genuine art. If, before an audience, we could fashion a proud, lovely rose, arrange each leaf, each petal until it is perfect, and then make it live even for an instant, it would be an unforgettable experience for all who watched. This is what must happen when we re-create music, when we make a composition live for a few minutes, for half an hour; the quality of living force must be there if our re-creation is to be meaningful.

Being human, we musicians can reflect only what we are, as in a mirror. Any affectation, or the slightest insincerity, instantly reveals itself as a sham.

We receive sparks of inspiration, store them carefully in our memories, and, when released, they fire our own re-creative power. I can relive the thrill I felt as a small child at Joseph Lhévinne's playing of *La Campanella* by Paganini-Liszt, at Ignaz Friedman's interpretation of Chopin's "Étude in Thirds," at Rachmaninoff's magical rendering of his Third Concerto, at the rich velvet tone of Mischa Elman's Concerto of Bruch. These are supreme moments in our lives because they affirm that we humble humans have the power to re-create living beauty.

By strong discipline, thorough training, broad and bold musical conceptions, we can capture this power to re-create.

Many personal factors go into the making of an artist: a high degree of imagination, intelligence, sensitivity, flexibility; the willingness to learn from every situation, to plod doggedly even when the going gets rugged; the courage of our artistic convictions even when fashionable musical-opinion-makers leave us in the minority. We must be stubborn optimists who will spend hours, weeks, even months working on dull problems of technique. Sometimes faith is the only thing to carry us over a veritable chasm of despair. Those of us who are inclined to daydream should train themselves to plod; those who plod too hard and dream too little should force themselves to relax and let their imagination roam freely. In a performance heart, mind, and hands all work together. The heart is filled to overflowing with wonder and beauty; the mind learns how to communicate these emotions; the hands must obediently and, under all conditions, execute the musical ideas that heart and mind command.

When we plant a seed to grow a flower we know its name, its color, shape, and approximate size at full bloom. We see it in our mind's eye taking its place in the garden setting we have chosen for it. Music-making isn't much different. We must be able to imagine every tone, every phrase, the whole composition as we wish it to sound, all the way to the grand sweep of the entire work; and we must be able to project it so that the listener receives precisely the impression we wish to create.

The rose you have planted in your garden will be beautiful at any time of day—in the early light of dawn, in the bright sun of noontime, in the blush of sunset, in the white light of the full moon. Likewise, in music, your recreation must always be convincing whether played on a spinet, a baby grand, a concert grand; whether in a living-room, a small theatre, a huge gymnasium, or outdoors.

We can even accept our own limitations and still be artists as long as we make the most of our possibilities from the very start. In art everything is worth while; art is luxury of the spirit. The smallest accomplishment is at least self-fulfilling and adds to our understanding of music and its beauty. Music is an integral part of living—a part of the air we breathe, a language more full of meaning than any spoken tongue. Communicative performance is the glorious beacon that can make even humdrum practicing a joy.

MUSIC IS A LANGUAGE

MUSIC IS a living language, more eloquent than any spoken tongue. The performer is the translator, the interpreter.

From the first note at our first lesson, all through our musical lives, we must aim at making every sound meaningful.

Most pianists play by ear. We never hear exactly how the music sounds as we play. We sit in front of the keyboard and sound emerges about four feet away, to the right of the open pianoforte. This is the spot toward which we should project our tone, where we should place ourselves as imaginary listeners. Franz Liszt once said that you must listen to yourself as critically as if you were a rival pianist in another room. Pianists often are so preoccupied with producing music that they forget about listening to it; this is why, to criticize constructively, we must imagine ourselves away from the pianoforte and concentrate on the continuous, meaningful flow of the musical line.

I like to practice with the pianoforte fully open and the music-rack down in order to give myself a feeling of space. In performance, when the pianoforte is open to reflect the tone into the auditorium, I look through the open space and find a place on which to concentrate my gaze. I imagine myself right there, listening. When I play with an orchestra, I usually play to one of the faces in the second-violin section. I try to express the subtlest nuance in every tone, to project it toward myself as audience. Once this becomes a habit, it will not be difficult to project toward a real audience of two thousand or twenty thousand, in a drawing-room, an auditorium, before a microphone. Wherever we are, we play for some definite listener at a definite place—ourselves—near the open pianoforte.

Mischa Elman, the violin virtuoso, felt that it is more important for the pianist than any other instrumentalist to practice the art of the uninterrupted melodic line. This is easier for singers and string players because they normally work with only one melody, while keyboard artists have a host of other factors to consider: two performing hands; two assisting feet; the problem of keeping the melody free from interference by harmonies and pedals. Sometimes it is a real effort to free a melody, to make it sing flowingly and shape its musical line in one unbroken sweep from beginning to end. Play your musical phrase and give your fullest, uninterrupted attention to the musical line. Be careful never to exaggerate the accent at the peak of the phrase or to let it get lost between a crescendo and a diminuendo; the musical line must flow naturally.

To establish the mood of a phrase, to blend it with its setting, to convey what we believe to be the precise meaning the composer wishes to express, is one of the greatest problems facing a pianist and one of the most thrilling adventures in a day's work. I have said that the language of music is the most eloquent of all, but it is also the most elusive, working by innuendo only, suggesting rather than stating, sometimes confusing us as to the composer's real intentions.

Here is a device that should be equally helpful to the beginner learning a Haydn minuet and the virtuoso reading, say, a Liszt rhapsody for the first time: use the spoken word as a master-key. Isolate the musical phrase; then tell yourself audibly, in plain language, what you think it was meant to express. Joy? Grief? Or homesickness, complaint, pain, gaiety, passion, foreboding? After you have decided on the most fitting verbal expression, experiment at the key-board until you succeed in establishing the mood musically. You will soon be able to convey the basic meaning, as you feel it, in musical terms; then develop it in every possible way. The melody sings forth imperturbably, but harmonies and the cautious use of the pedal assist you.

I remember how Rachmaninoff explained to me the problem of phrasing: he showed me an elastic band and stretched it slightly, then allowed it to bounce back; next, he stretched it beyond a certain point, and it snapped. He meant to say that no part of a musical line should be stretched out of proportion to the whole composition. We have a natural tendency to take a breath, so to speak, after each phrase, but we must be careful not to overdo it. Actually the end of one phrase should prepare the listener for the next, or at least blend into it so that the musical fabric remains strong and whole. There are even instances in which a whole series of phrases leads to a sort of gateway opening up a new mood; almost as if another light had been turned on—for example, the E♭ major chord in bar 21 of the second movement of Chopin's F-minor Concerto.

This brings us to the very stringent problem of diminuendo: for some reason it tempts us to slow down, but diminuendo only means diminished sonority and must not interfere with the rhythmic pulse of the music. A pianist who reduces tempo together with volume is either a beginner or a bad musician. Chopin felt so strongly about this that he recommended always to practice with the metronome.

Whatever the tone volume, a ritardando must be smooth,

almost imperceptible. Casals compared it to an automobile stopping at a red light: "If you stop abruptly, you fall forward and break your skull. Slow down gradually so that everything remains in place and you can get out of your car with dignity." Ritardandi must be as gentle as possible. Only the pianist must know that they are there at all.

Usually, as we grow older, the relationship to our repertoire matures; our ideas of what a particular phrase, a particular composition, should express become more complex. Take the opening theme of the last movement of Chopin's F-minor Concerto, which Huneker called "Mazurka-like, very graceful, and full of pure sweet melody."

When I first learned it I was about twelve years old. I played it in its most straightforward manner, with simple peasant gaiety. A few years later I gave it more polish and put the gaiety in a more elegant setting; I had come to feel in it echoes of the aristocracy of Chopin and his Parisian audiences. For many concerts this seemed to me the correct interpretation. Then, after a period of years, I discovered a note of complaint that changed the character of the gay theme and gave it a new element of drama. This was a fascinating process that I experienced many times. As we grow with a musical work we constantly seek and find new nuances, new details, new meanings, and whatever we accepted in the past appears as a mere half-truth to which we can never return.

I never make notes in my scores. I like to start afresh at every relearning. Perhaps some minute detail not noticed before or not fully understood will give an entirely new meaning to a phrase.

Creation is life, so re-creation must also be alive. Life is movement. Clouds float, leaves stir in the breeze. Our organs, our glands, are in motion even while we sleep, the moment they stop we are dead. A brook that stops flowing becomes a stagnant pool. A melody without direction becomes purposeless.

Most great music was written according to definite architectural lines; each small detail has its place, from the first sound to the last.

When we examine a phrase we see many things in it as a phrase unit. When we combine it with the next phrase, its connotation changes completely, for we are looking at a two-phrase unit. Longer compositions should be divided into sections as long as possible, so that each phrase receives correct dimensions.

Every section is a musical paragraph like a prose paragraph, the meaning of which can usually be summed up in a few words. Each has a point toward which the music builds and from which it recedes. Some music builds all the way to the last note, i.e., the Fugue from Bach's *Chromatic Fantasia and Fugue*. Generally, however, melody moves like the ebb and flow of an ocean tide; many small waves help to build up to a mighty climax, then subside again and become absorbed by the expanse of rolling water. See, for example, Chopin's Étude, Opus 10, No. 3, in E major.

But there is also miniature music, intimate music. Here a tiny dynamic scale and phrase are in order, with a view to daintiness rather than grandeur. Again, we must look for the direction of the basic melody, for the climax of each section, each phrase. Every detail has to fit into its setting. A *sfz* in a Schubert waltz is an entirely different *sfz* from that in a Brahms concerto.

To sum up, here are three basic rules:

1. Concentrate for the full length of the musical line, without interruption.

2. Determine the mood to be expressed and make every detail point toward it.

3. Find the focal point or climax of a phrase or section in order to give direction to your musical thought.

Beauty of sound is another pianistic virtue that must be acquired from the very start. The great composers for the keyboard placed much emphasis on the quality of tone. Debussy gave a rather sweeping order: "Every sound must be beautiful." Chopin insisted that one should always practice on the best pianoforte available and keep it in perfect tune to accustom the ear to the finest possible sound.

Even when we practice scales the sound can be beautiful. We must never forget the infinite variety of tonal shading we are able to produce, the variations of touch, of which there are thousands. The shaping and mixing of sound are our most personal contribution to the re-creative process. "Nuances are the musician's palette," said Liszt. "His hand must master them completely, so they are at his beck and call." As nothing else, they reveal the pianist's personality.

Even a child learning his first piece can be helped to project his personality. I suggest he sings the melody away from the pianoforte; if this is difficult at first, the teacher might write it out on paper, illustrate the phrase as exactly as possible, indicate where to sing loudly or softly, where to place an accent, where to increase or diminish. As the child first learns by imitation, he will lose his inhibitions, and suddenly his own reactions will come flooding into the little piece of music, young as he might be. He will learn the naturalness of the rise and fall of a phrase because he will have to breathe as he sings; then at the pianoforte he will simply transfer what he has learned and the melody will come alive.

Always a student must be admonished to make technical

exercises sound beautiful: to use crescendo and diminuendo, to listen to his sound, to polish his tones, to aim at an even quality. At first the tonal palette will be meager, even crude; new students tend to use either *pp* or *ff* just as the novice painter works at first only with the primary colours. Normally the pianist's first showpiece gets the biggest acclaim when played in the *f* to *ff* range, so that end of the dynamic scale is usually explored first. (As Moriz Rosenthal once quipped: "As long as you've got to play the pianoforte, do it loud and fast.")

Then someone may tactfully suggest that the pupil is playing too forcefully, at which he may flee to the opposite end of the dynamic scale and explore *pp* to *p*. It takes time to come to terms with the many variations of touch and sound.

Once as a child I played a Chopin nocturne for Alfred Cortot. He said: "This was no good, and you know it. Play it again as if you were the teacher showing me how to play." I played it again and he was satisfied. This taught me a most important lesson. It was the beginning of my campaign for what I call "exercises in imagination."

Through exercises in imagination the novice will learn variety of touch.

Instead of telling him merely, "Play louder," or "Play softer," I tell him, "Sound happier," or "Try a melancholy undertone." Instead of saying, "Put more forearm strength into this note," I might tell him to put more warmth of feeling into the passage. Everybody has a different physical solution to a given tonal problem, depending on the size and strength of hands and arms, and on previous experience.

I make sure that the student avoids muscular tenseness and look out for weak spots in his technique to be repaired by appropriate exercises; otherwise I let him find his own physical solution, almost like the boy Mozart, who once used his nose to push down a key in a chord he could not span.

With exercises in imagination the pupil stops playing mere notes; he is making music, his sounds conveying meaning to the listener. When a small child learns his first gavotte, minuet, waltz, the teacher might take him by the hand, lead him off the pianoforte stool into the room, and let him *dance* to the music so that he *feels* what he is trying to express. Once a child experiences this freedom of movement, he can transfer it to the music, just as he transferred to the keyboard his first experience of singing a melodic line.

A child's dormant imagination might go to waste unless developed by the teacher. By feeling and doing small things, imaginative powers can eventually face enormous projects.

3

CONCEPTS OF PROPORTION,
TEMPO, RHYTHM

To CREATE and sustain a mood is a delicate procedure—the net that casts the spell, that holds the audience. Without "mood" the finest performance remains but a reproduction of notes, black-and-white sound-pictures untouched by human warmth, that may command respect but will never capture the imagination. It is the adventure of the unknown, the vast imponderable area created by the questions whether we have chosen the right mood for our interpretation, and how we communicate it to the audience, that supplies the personal touch, makes a concert interesting, exciting, alive.

The art of re-creation is full of seeming contradictions. A performance must sound fresh and spontaneous, almost improvised; yet every tone, every nuance, the slightest pause, the most furtive slur, must be the result of careful, endless study and experiment.

Every masterpiece is based on an architectural plan. This iş its steel skeleton into which we fill the mass of detail, inflection, accent. We don't always fill it in quite the same manner. We practice in order to develop flexibility, sensitivity, maximum mastery of our instrument. But also, practice gives us the only sure footing in a sea of imponderables.

Rhythm is the basic pulse of a composition; tempo, its pace. A steady rhythmic pulse can be developed with hard practice, but tempo remains arbitrary. We have no proper vocabulary to indicate exact rates of speed, beyond such generalities as *largo* (broad), *andante* (walking), *vivace* (lively), *allegro* (happy), *presto* (fast), *grave* (serious), and many more, most of which are indicative of mood rather than of motion. No two artists use precisely the same tempo in a given composition; hardly any artist uses precisely the same tempo every time he plays the same piece. Actually it may vary slightly from one instrument to another because, to maintain the proper mood, we must exploit the possibilities of every instrument to best advantage.

A student's *presto,* for example, may sound very fast because he will play as fast as he can manage and his efforts to hurry become evident; but when an artist uses the same tempo it might sound slow, since he has perfect control of his hands and *sounds* controlled, while the student *sounds* hurried. This is why I recommend use of the metronome from the very beginning, from the very first scale, throughout our musical lives. I still use it daily, even on tour, to maintain the discipline of daily practice and full mastery of the keyboard, even when the keyboards vary. The best kind is the electric metronome because it is built so that one can more accurately regulate the rate at which to increase the speed. I prefer to increase speed by regular intervals such as twos, threes, fours, fives and sixes. Perhaps I will start at 60 and proceed metronomically to 62, 64, 66 etc. Later I will start at 60 and proceed by threes: 60, 63, 66, 69 etc. Still later I'll proceed by 4's: 60, 64, 68, 72 etc. Then by fives: 60, 65, 70, 75, 80. This assures a much more even control of speed.

Proportion is the elusive cousin of architecture. It is one of the most difficult, and one of the basic, problems of a pianist. Tempo, rhythm, dynamics, mood—all these elements must have been explored before we can hope to attain the ideal proportion. We can establish the "right" tempo only if we realize what would be too fast or too slow. We arrive at controlled tone-colour only if we know what is too loud or too soft. Exaggeration and understatement, constant probing of detail, alone will teach us to project all shades of mood.

First, we must know how to approach a passage technically. Just as we wear different kinds of coats for different kinds of weather, we use a different technique for every mood. Cortot recommends a light, quick, almost staccato fingertip touch for passages of rapid fingerwork, and a flat, ball-of-the-finger caress of the keys for slow legato. There are a thousand secrets of touch that a pianist's ear can teach.

Robert Schumann felt that the cultivation of the ear was of prime importance. In his "Rules and Maxims for Young Musicians" he tells them to endeavour in good time to listen to the sounds around them—the doorbell, the windowpane, the cuckoo—and to discover which tones and note they produce. Every pianoforte requires a slightly different touch; every room in which we play requires different volume.

Chopin practiced a great deal of Mozart and Bach during his formative years to acquire a sensitive touch. Mozart sonatas are ideal to develop the p to mp to mf to f area of dynamics. Bach's original works for keyboard, especially the fugues, require the most coordination from hand and mind, and I suggest devoting one hour daily to their practice; they teach us finger control so that we can play many voices at once, keeping them separate, clear, and expressive, yet within the fabric of the whole composition; this background in polyphonic thinking will always be useful. Rachmaninoff recommended Scarlatti as an invigorating "cold bath" for finger technique. After I had had a ten-day vacation from the pianoforte, he put me on an exclusive diet of Scarlatti sonatas for three weeks in order to recondition my touch.

Franz Liszt had a method of practicing that is worth noting because it was the foundation for the revolutionary technique that established him as the "father of modern pianism". He was not yet twenty, living in Paris, when he was overawed by Paganini's phenomenal virtuosity and pledged himself to achieve on the keyboard what this man achieved on four strings. He developed his method by himself and submitted himself to a merciless drill of his fingers six hours a day:

Octaves in scales for two hours to make his fingers both strong and supple; he lifted his hands high and attacked the keys with full energy. The same for chords and arpeggios.

Repetition of notes, octaves, and chords on the same key for muscular control; trills, with the other three fingers resting on the keys.

He was careful not to move arms and shoulders, or to bend his head forward; he sat straight and bent his head backward, but very slightly.

New pieces were studied in five stages. He started by reading very slowly, four or five times, each time from a different viewpoint. First only the notes; secondly, note values; thirdly, nuances, changes in expression; fourthly, analyzing bass and descant, always searching for melodies that could be accentuated; finally he decided on the tempi. Then he began to practice: he analyzed his own emotional reactions and, after passionate passages, would proceed as if indifferent or tired to express the natural slackening of feeling after an emotional storm. He insisted that passionate self-abandon to the music had to dictate a pianist's interpretation, but he had to have perfect physical control of his hands. "Never must your fingers stand in the way of your artistic interpretation," Carl Czerny, his own teacher, had always said to him.

When I study a new piece, I start to practice very slowly with the metronome to get it comfortably and accurately into my fingers; and I play it slowly until I have the feeling of perfect control. Forcing speed too soon is like forcing a child to walk before he is ready. You make no progress, and you can jeopardize the equilibrium and control you may have acquired.

In my steadily growing repertoire I find that every piece of music has its price, in terms of effort to get it under control. There is no passage so difficult that it would not be possible to find a metronome speed slow enough to play it comfortably. We must train the mind before we train our hands; and the mind first reacts against adding new patterns to its subconscious; so we have to placate it, cajole it, prove that the new pattern can be easy—which we achieve by working at a slow tempo. Once the composition is acquired, our memory will retain it, and we have plenty of time to play it as fast as we want.

Once I know a passage thoroughly at a slow tempo, I take it a little faster, generally only two metronome numbers, so that the mind and hands hardly notice the change. At each playing I increase the speed by two metronome numbers until I reach a limit where I can still deliver the passage accurately but can't exceed that speed. There I stop.

At the next practice period I start all over again from the original slow tempo, which already seems considerably easier than a few hours before. If it feels very much easier, I advance at the rate of three metronome numbers, taking care, however, that the fingers don't feel the strain. I never go beyond the point of tension; this point advances by itself, day by day, week by week, without forcing, until I reach a point far beyond the speed I need. Yet, I still start slowly every day and seldom exceed a five-number advancement rate, because the muscles would feel the strain and the foundations of the kinesthetic response that I am trying to build might be shaken. At times this way of practicing seems monotonous, but I have found that the time spent is well invested. Incidentally, I learned it from Rachmaninoff, who felt it was the only way to gain firm fingers.

Sometimes it happens to me, as to every pianist, that I have real difficulty with a passage. Then I simply put it away for some time. When I revive it I am sometimes amazed to see to what degree my earlier work bears fruit. The piece suddenly seems easier, my playing surer, more accurate. It is as if it had been germinating all by itself.

I have given considerable thought to the pros and cons of metronome drill; that is, to the extent to which it should be used.

I have found that it gives best results when done every day. It is useful not only to maintain rhythm, but also for finger-work, octave work, jump passages, even memorizing, for it relieves the mind of the mechanical necessity of counting time. I am a slow memorizer and have experimented with different procedures, none of them as effective in the long run. The different speeds force us to hear the same passage in many different ways, thus helping us to free it from the printed paper and fixing every tiny detail in our minds. Daily we become stronger as we work from beginning to end, from slow to almost concert tempo, improving our mental and technical grasp, always smoothing away rough spots. On really complicated, stubborn passages I practice three times at each metronome speed, in the following manner:

(1) right hand *f* with left hand *p*;
(2) left hand *f* with right hand *p*;
(3) both hands in proper proportion.

I have yet to find a problem that could not be solved, partly at least, by metronome drill.

I always aim at a faster tempo than I will need. In performance it should never be necessary to use your ability to the limits; there should always be a margin of reserve. Here again, one of Rachmaninoff's truisms: "If you want a horse to run a mile-long race, train him to run a mile and a half; then the mile will be easy."

On the other hand, the metronome is only a means to an end, a tool. It should never be considered more than that. While it helps us to gain freedom from technical problems and to acquire the "margin of reserve," we have to learn in good time to acquire freedom from the metronome itself. To me the metronome is like the chrysalis that protects the insect until it has grown into a butterfly. We must use the metronome to good advantage but not become its prisoner.

First there was freedom from technical problems, then freedom from the metronome; finally there is freedom from the keyboard, so essential for technical assuredness as well as beautiful tone. If our hands are "glued" to the keyboard, afraid of losing notes or hand position, our tone will become monotonous and sound as unfree as we actually are. In order to free the hands I suggest making exercises of such compositions as the following:

> Bach—Invention No. 8, F major;
> Chopin—Trois Écossaises;
> Brahms—Hungarian Dance No. 1;
> Debussy—Prelude: Tierces Alternées.

I have selected these at random, out of many hundreds equally good. They are of medium difficulty and exploit all kinds of tonal approaches that are best attained when the hands are free to fly above the keyboard.

Exaggerate hand motion as you practice. If you need visual

help, mark arrows pointing downward at the beginning of each phrase and arrows pointing up at the end of each phrase. The "down" arrow should remind the student not just to press down the key with the finger but to use the weight of the arms to establish the timbre. The "up" arrow means, "Throw your hands up, wrists first, one foot above the keys." All staccatos except finger staccato and all rests require this movement during slow practice. If this becomes a habit, your music will not stay "in the piano;" your hands, your sounds, your musical concepts will be free, and your music will soar.

I realize that this is difficult for the beginner. The pianoforte is a complex instrument, an orchestra within itself. Sit-

"Comfortable position at the keyboard: shoulders and elbows down, wrists slightly up so that hands are relaxed."

ting in front of this massive piece of furniture, the neophyte is tempted to hang on to it to gain confidence, to lean on it, clutch at it, hit it with all his strength—and the pianoforte, being a sensitive instrument, hits back; it exposes the young pianist's inexperience by sounding harsh, uneven, ragged, unpolished—just as the nervousness of a singer or string player is betrayed by uncontrolled vibrato. The student must learn that the pianoforte is his friend and ally, his medium to express whatever he wants to say if he handles it properly.

Whenever hands are raised off the keyboard for rests or phrase endings, wrists should be *up* with the hands hanging in order to insure relaxation. If this becomes habitual you will have endurance even in a difficult composition.

"Hands should be raised wrists up. A raised wrist at every phrase ending and rest insures relaxed hands that will perform during endurance tests."

4

MORE ABOUT PRACTICING

LEOPOLD GODOWSKY made a fine distinction between technique and mechanism: speed, fingerwork, octaves, according to him, fall into the latter category; they are separate problems, tools, while technique is all-conclusive. Technique implies complete mastery of the keyboard, including the ability to produce beautiful tone, to use the pedal sensitively, to memorize.

We must think of our pianoforte as if it were part of us, or, rather, an extension of our equipment to express musical thought. Being a mechanical instrument, it is not the composer's medium; *that* honor is reserved for us who play. The audience must not even be conscious of the instrument; therefore, neither must we. We cannot play for an audience unless, or until, we have confidence in ourselves. In a way a concert artist is like a ski champion, who cannot expect to win unless he has complete command over the two pieces of wood attached to his feet; or like an actor who must completely submerge himself in his characterization to make it convincing. A musician cannot give a good performance unless he can forget about his instrument. Technical mastery should not be considered an accomplishment in itself; it is the *sine qua non* of a virtuoso, the lowest rung of the ladder, the basic necessity, the starting point.

Chances are that three-quarters of your repertoire will contain passages too difficult or awkward to be learned by practising merely scales and arpeggios. We all have some little *bête noire* over which we stumble, and even though it may not throw us, it jars us and makes us expend so much thought and energy that we cannot concentrate properly on the rest of the composition.

Many technical exercise books have been written by Carl Czerny, Charles-Louis Hanon, Johann Pischna, and others, for the purpose of training the fingers to overcome stumbling blocks in certain pieces. All this, however, solves only part of the problem. When you have done the work, you will know the exercises, but not the passage. The only solution is to make a special study of each little problem as it comes up, isolate it, turn it into an exercise and, after you have conquered the difficulty, put it back into the context of the composition.

Here is a list with subsequent illustrations:

Fingerwork cadenzas;
Short technical passages;
Staccato octaves, sixths;
Chord jumps;
Repeated notes;
Ornamentation;
Trills;
Cadenza runs in rhythmic framework;
Polyrhythms;
Fingering;
Pedalling.

In Chopin's E major Nocturne the final cadenza is a rapid cantilena passage; work on it all by itself, in shifting accents, and later with the metronome, starting slowly and increasing in speed, as outlined in the previous chapter.

Illustrations for "shifting accents":

(a) -... -... -... -... etc.
(b) .-.. .-.. .-.. .-.. etc.
(c) ..-. ..-. ..-. ..-. etc.
(d) ...- ...- ...- ...- etc.

This principle is applicable to any finger passage and can be adapted to any rhythm. For example, use a six-note group for the entire last movement of Beethoven's Sonata, Opus 32, No. 2, or a three-note group for Bach's D minor Prelude from the *Well-Tempered Clavier,* Book 1.

Or take the passage as in Schubert's *Moment Musical* in F minor, ninth bar. Work at it very slowly, carefully pressing each key down to the very bottom; then transpose it and make a regular exercise of it (illustration). Soon you will feel comfortable with the passage and won't have to think of it as a problem when you play the piece.

Another problem, in Schumann's *Papillons,* requires knowledge of keyboard reaction to hand bounce (Illustration). Mastering this, you will have acquired a skill that you can carry over to a great many similar problems, such as even the difficult octave passages in Liszt's *Hungarian Rhapsody No. 6.*

Illustrations of difficult passages made into finger exercises to solve specific problems: the first is from Bar 9 in Schubert's *Moment Musical* in F minor, the second from Bar 6 of the Polonaise, Section No. 11, in Schumann's *Papillons*. Such exercises should be practiced at metronome speeds gradually increasing from very slow to the correct tempo. The bounce your hands acquire in the Schumann can be used in various places; the same muscles are used when playing longer sustained passages of octaves and intervals such as the octave runs in the last movement of Beethoven's "Waldstein" Sonata, or the opening bars of the scherzo in Chopin's B♭ minor Sonata.

"Firm octave mold; middle fingers are curved underneath while rigid thumb and little finger strike octave cleanly on the piano."*

When you play staccato octaves, such as those in the opening passage of Mendelssohn's G minor Concerto, make your hand into a stiff "octave mold," as I call it; the middle fingers curled under so that they will be out of the way. If you keep your hand in this position you will have clean, firm octaves, no matter where you put it down. In order to acquire this new habit, you might play octave scales in all the major and minor keys, slow to fast, with the metronome for a few days, until you get the feel of it. Then move this new skill back into the context of the concerto. This firm "mold" concept is useful for sixths, thirds, or any other interval used in rapid

staccato passages such as the scales in sixths in the last movement of Saint-Saëns's G minor Concerto. When you have long
octave passages that require endurance, such as the left-hand
octave section in Chopin's Polonaise, Opus 53, and the right-
hand passages in Liszt's Hungarian Rhapsody No. 6, you must
work with the metronome very slowly and repeat the passage
four times (without stopping) at each metronome speed from
slow to fast, in order to build up the necessary power of endurance. You will suffer physical pain and learn to endure it.
You will emerge in the end invigorated with a tremendous
margin of reserve, and with the knowledge of complete
mastery, which is well worth the effort.

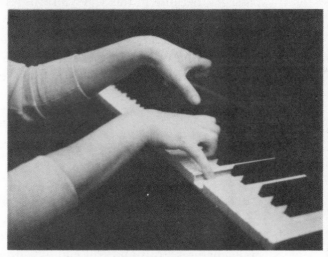

"Octave mold
off piano."

A passage requiring accurate jumping of the hands from
one part of the keyboard to another requires help from the eyes.
Practice very slowly and use the metronome. Don't look at
the center of the keyboard but at the keys you wish to strike at
the extreme right or left. Sometimes both hands have to jump
simultaneously in opposite directions (as in the final chord
bars of the bravura section from the scherzo of Chopin's B♭

minor Sonata). Practice hands separately at first; then, when you put both hands together, look at the weaker one—at the left if you are right-handed, and at the right if you are left-handed. Take two of the leaps and repeat back and forth until you can hit accurately ten times consecutively, then the next two, etc. If you continue to have trouble, use the "junior developer formula" (illustrated on p. 44) on this type of passage. This problem takes patience, time, and effort at the first learning, though much less at each relearning.

When you come across a passage of repeated notes, as in Chopin's Grande Valse Brillante No. 1, make an exercise of it. I always recommend changing fingers on fast repeated-note passages, because in this way you will rely on fingers rather than on piano action. Practice this exercise for a while on the closed keyboard lid by tapping the fingering out with correct accent on the wood to get the *feel* of the passage. When it sounds right here, it will be easier to make it sound right on the keys.

Exercise for repeated notes.

I learned to perform mordents, appoggiaturas, crossed appoggiaturas, trills and trill endings, turns, and all sorts of fussy ornamentation in this way: Play the desired mordent, trill ending, or whatever pattern is difficult, four times in C major, four times in D flat major, four times in D major, etc., all the way up and down the chromatic scale. Learn to do mordents with all possible fingerings: 132, 232, 243, 343, 354, 454, and in both hands. You are teaching necessary patterns to the muscles.

In the same way, going up and down the chromatic scale, trills should be practiced with every possible finger combination: 13, 23, 24, 34, 35, 45; same procedure for the left hand. A slight loose-wrist motion is desirable. A four-finger trill combination (1323) is not recommended, because it puts too much responsibility on the fingers alone. Use the metronome, slowly at first, perhaps only four notes at a beat of 80; always aim at steadiness rather than speed.

etc.

In the following trill exercise, the bottom note should simply be held while the upper note is struck in a hammerlike combination of arm and finger. This is done by leaning the hand toward the silent side for each struck note. This causes arm rotation which will be the eventual basis for the trill. This exercise should be done with every possible trill finger-

ing (13, 23, 24, 34, 35, 45) on all degrees of the chromatic
scale.

After you have mastered the above exercise, try holding
down the top note (silent D) and proceed to strike C as
measured above. Proceed on all degrees of the chromatic
scale. Use a metronome to beat on each quarter at a very
slow rate. Gradually, daily, start at the same slow level and
raise your speed by small steps.

When there is a long cadenza in one hand while the other
hand maintains the rhythm, I count the number of notes in
the cadenza and divide the total by the number of beats it
must fill. I practice with exaggerated accents on the notes
where the beats should fall until I get the feel of the rhythm.
Chopin's Prelude, Opus 28, No. 18, is a good example. Simi-
larly, when the piano has a recitative against an orchestral
accompaniment, as in the second movements of Liszt's Concerto No. 1 and Chopin's Concerto No. 2, the soloist and conductor sometimes establish imaginary accents as anchors until
they have performed the work together so many times that
such anchors are no longer necessary.

Polyrhythm is another difficult problem with an easy, if
painstaking, solution. The best way to get the feel of two
against three, or three against four, is to begin with a hand
exercise: simply beat out the rhythms on a table with your

hands while counting aloud.

HAND EXERCISE FOR 2 AGAINST 3

Count 1 2 *and* 3 in a Slow-Quick-Quick-Slow cadence. In this exercise, note that on the count of 1, both hands strike the table; on 2 just the right hand; on *and* just the left hand, and on 3, just the right.

Right Hand	—	— —		—	— —
Count	1	2 and 3		1	2 and 3
Left Hand	—	—		—	—

After mastering the above hand exercise, proceed to the following piano exercise.

PIANO EXERCISE FOR 2 AGAINST 3

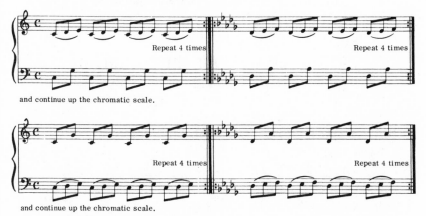

and continue up the chromatic scale.

and continue up the chromatic scale.

An effective way to learn how to play three against four is to use the phrase "Pass the golden butter." This phrase is ideal because when one pronounces the syllables naturally, the proper cadence becomes automatic. When doing the following hand exercise use the words of this phrase instead of counting by numbers. Also, it is best to start with the syllables in the word "golden." After beating these syllables in a slow cadence, add the word butter, the syllables of which fall naturally into a quick cadence. Continue adding the words as shown below until the entire phrase is mastered.

HAND EXERCISES FOR 3 AGAINST 4

LH RH
Gold - en
SLOW

LH RH   LH RH
Gold - en   But - ter
SLOW SLOW QUICK

RH   LH RH   LH RH
The   Gold - en   But - ter
QUICK   SLOW SLOW QUICK

RH
and
LH   RH   LH RH   LH RH
Pass   The   Gold - en   But - ter
SLOW   QUICK SLOW SLOW QUICK

PIANO EXERCISES FOR 3 AGAINST 4

Repeat 4 times   Repeat 4 times

and continue the exercise all the way up and down the scale at half-step intervals.

Repeat 4 times   Repeat 4 times

and continue all the way up and down the scale at half-step intervals.

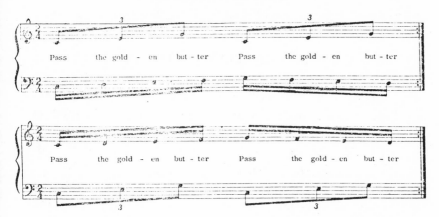

Fingering has made big strides since the days of Karl Philipp Emanuel Bach, who in his *True Art of Playing Keyboard Instruments* recommended for scales the fingering 1234512345, etc., instead of the then conventional 121212! But it is impossible to give set fingering rules for any given passage, because what is easy for a small hand may be awkward for a larger one. Personally, I recommend maintaining a similar fingering where a note pattern is repeated, so that the hands can keep to a set routine. A good illustration is in Bach's C minor Prelude, of the *Well-Tempered Clavier,* Book 1, beginning with bar 28. The right hand plays an eight-note pattern eight times, using the same fingering regardless of hand position: 32343231. In the same way the left hand repeats its pattern, using the same fingering regardless of hand position: 23212324. This principle eliminates the tendency to unconscious accents and is much simpler to memorize.

Whenever possible, use fingering to improve legato. Here is a legato fingering for what would otherwise be an extremely rough passage: bar 2 of the *Un poco animato* section of the first movement of Saint-Saëns's Concerto No. 2 in G minor:

54 45 4543 4343 4535 4543 4343 2343 4534|5̄

32 12 1221 2121 2312 1221 2121 121 2312|3

Experiment with awkward passages and try every possibility. There is no law that says the thumb can't be used on
black keys, or that the third and fourth fingers cannot follow
the fifth in an ascending scale in the right hand or a descending scale in the left hand. For example, the last bars of
Chopin's "Étude in Sixths" are easily negotiated by the conventional back-finger chromatic-scale fingering, with the
thumb staccato on all the bottom notes. Get as much into a
hand span as possible.

Examples: Chopin Prelude No. 6 left hand theme; 54321.
Use mirror fingering where practical. Example: Chopin Prelude No. 3, last three quarters

        Right Hand   2341   2341   2345   4
        Left Hand   4321   4321   4321   2

Notice how Right Hand and Left Hand thumbs come down
together.

In legato chord passages try to keep at least the melody line
legato. Lean on it with your fingers, legato, while you pick
up the other notes demi-marcato. Never depend on the pedal
to do the work of the fingers. The second movement of
Beethoven's "Pathétique" Sonata is a good illustration.

The pedal should be used only to enhance the harmonic
effect and to help to bind the legato that the fingers can't
manage. For best effect use it as little as possible. Never use
the pedal when you can do without it. In pedalling, the ear is
the only guide, since every pianoforte reacts differently to it.
In legato chord passages the pedal should be changed
immediately *after* the chord is played. Practice this very slowly
until the principle is understood. Chopin's Prelude No. 20,

in C minor, is a good example. There are places in Debussy and in Busoni's arrangements of Bach's organ compositions where use of the *sostenuto* pedal is effective; but don't become too dependent on it, as some leading makes of European pianofortes don't have this. In bars 42 - 45 of Debussy's "Cathédral Engloutie" re-play the first chords silently, keep hands down, lift pedal to recapture sound. The opening chords of this Prelude should be played legato with fingers as well as with pedal to encourage horizontal line. For people who are cultivating the *pp* to *p* dynamic range it is useful to practice Mozart and Haydn sonatas completely with soft pedal so that the ear is forced to work with a very low dynamic ceiling. This is not meant for performance, of course.

For really stubborn passages involving long finger work and octaves I use what I call "developers," because they build the passage in the hands and develop endurance at the same time. Here is the formula:

Take the first eight notes, accent the *ninth,* which is your pivot, after which you return to the beginning. Repeat four times. Then start on the *second* note, use the *tenth* note for a pivot, go back to the second, and repeat four times. Then start with the *third* note, etc., until the end of the passage.

Formula for "developers" using a C major scale as a model.

This can be used on the entire last movement of the B♭ minor Chopin Sonata; on the fingerwork and octave passages in the last movement of the Tschaikovsky Concerto No. 1; on the octave work at the end of the Liszt Sonata.

Formula for "junior developers" using a chromatic scale in octaves as a model.

For short but difficult passages I use a "junior" version of developers. Repeat the first two notes in semi-quavers for four crotchets. Proceed with the second and third notes for four crotchets, proceed with the third and fourth notes, etc., to the end of the passage. Then start at the beginning, play the first two notes, add the *third* as a pivot, return, repeat four times. Start with the *second* note, use the *fourth* as a pivot, repeat four times. Start with the *third* note, etc., to the end of the passage.

Next phase:

Start again with the first note of the passage and use the *fifth* note as a pivot.

Start again, and use the *seventh* note as a pivot.

The grouping of nine notes is the largest maneuverable group for this kind of passage development. This can be used in such complicated passages as the tenth variation of Schumann's *Études Symphoniques,* or the scale in fourths in the first movement of Chopin's B minor Sonata.

Dull, time-consuming work! But such daily practice over a period of time will almost guarantee absolute perfection at every performance. The possibility of becoming "derailed" is almost nil.

Don't exaggerate the pause—it should hardly break the rhythmic pulse. Resist the temptation to take undue advantage of it.

I recommend playing all repeats marked by the composer. In scherzi, architecture demands it; in sonatas, only impatience denies it. Music is not a hurried affair if the composer thought a repeat necessary for the full absorption of his music, obey him! You are familiar with every note, but your listeners may be glad of a second chance to recognize themes.

Try not to place undue emphasis on unimportant parts of the music. It can distract from really important material.

Never play a phrase twice in exactly the same way. Examine the context in which the twin phrases appear, and use your imagination if there are no composer's markings to establish their direction. Sometimes a softer imitation of the first phrase is appropriate. At other times both phrases are steps toward a greater climax. The composer meant to emphasize mood by repetition; define it. Examples are Chopin's

Ballade No. 4 and Haydn's Variations in F minor.

When you have a tremolo or repeated accompaniment figure, create an effect with the whole passage rather than awareness of individual notes. Examples are, the left-hand octave tremolo in the first movement of Beethoven's "Pathétique Sonata" and the right-hand figuration in Rachmaninoff's Prelude in G# minor.

However, before assigning an accompaniment figure to the role of mood-setter, be sure that it is not a melody in its own right. In the first movement of Beethoven's Sonata, Opus 14, No. 1, the arpeggio figures are so important melodically that use of pedal cannot be recommended because this would cloud their lyrical clarity.

Small hands often find it necessary to roll or break a chord. If you are in this position—as I am—you will have to find a way of doing it in a manner that will not impair the music. Remember that besides breaking a chord from left to right (bottom to top) it can be done the other way around if it agrees better with the context of the music. Better still, play as many solid notes as possible *on the beat,* the remaining notes *afterward,* so that the essential rhythm won't be disturbed. For example, in the opening chords of Rachmaninoff's Second Concerto, play the left thumb quietly after all the other notes have been struck simultaneously.

Both portamento- and rounded-phrase-types of legato should be cultivated. Each has its place and sometimes the quality of a piano's touch will require you to interchange them. When I was studying Chopin's F minor Nocturne, Opus 55, No. 1, for the first time, Cortot recommended a portamento-type legato with the full weight of the wrist and hand resting separately on each tone, while Rachmaninoff recommended a rounded-phrase legato emanating from the fingertips and guided by the wrist and elbow (like tracing a

semicircle) so that the tone would float in one circular arc
from the beginning to the very end of the phrase. Both
methods produced good results, and only the pianist can decide which type of legato to use. For instance, in Schumann's
"Strange Lands and People," from *Scenes from Childhood,*
the lyrical style definitely calls for the rounded-phrase legato,
while in Schubert's Impromptu in A flat major the portamento
type seems more appropriate. Turn the hand to emphasize
a legato interval; the larger the interval, the larger the air
space between hand and keyboard.

"Left hand pre-
pares melody note:
Turn hands so that
there is air space
between fingers
and keys—the
larger the melodic
interval, the
larger the air space
should be. In this
way you gain con-
trol of sound."

Memorizing should be such an integral part of the absorbing process of learning a new composition that it happens
spontaneously, without forcing. However, if you have to
speed the memory process, you can work on the section to be
memorized first thing in the morning when your mind is fresh,
and review it thoroughly for a half hour at the end of each
practice period, and always before bedtime. Sometimes, if the
problem is particularly knotty, it is helpful to take the music to
bed and review it mentally, playing and hearing the notes in
your mind with occasional glances at the score. While you

sleep, what you have been learning will settle in your subconscious.

Ear training is very important, and more people than we
realize have absolute or relative pitch that can be developed.
Only about two per cent of the population is biologically tone-
deaf. The trained listener has a decided advantage in learning
music; every effort should be made to develop the inner and
outer listening abilities. Nadia Boulanger made me work all
my harmony lessons away from the pianoforte in order to
develop the capacities of my inner ear. At first we must train
our consciousness of rhythm and melodic curve by singing
the melody we are learning. Later, when we start to play
polyphonic music, we can sing or hum one melody while we
play the other. When we learn a concerto we can sing important cues, in places where the solo instrument has to
accompany or blend with the orchestra.

Practicing a concerto, the pianist must realize that, whatever the quality or size of the orchestra with which he plays
—whether it is one of the great ensembles of the world, a
student orchestra, or an amateur group—performing a concerto is a collaboration. You cannot play the work alone. You
must earn the orchestra's respect for your musical concept
and must make them want to work with you, not against you.
It is rarely the orchestra's or the conductor's fault when the
results are not to the pianist's satisfaction. Try to sing the
orchestral parts; this will help you to listen to the orchestra.
Talk to the conductor about your interpretation and mark
what he has to say; you will learn things of great importance
by this communication of thoughts. A good conductor is a
most highly trained listener, sometimes better equipped to
help you in your interpretation than teachers or colleagues.
Before rehearsals start, discuss special problems with your
conductor and you will both adjust and blend your thoughts

to the benefit of the joint production. Let the conductor control his men and don't interfere; they are his instrument as the pianoforte is yours. But help him. Watch him.

Keeping our own abilities in their proper perspective with our concepts, as compared with other artists' abilities, is extremely important. "Thou shalt not covet thy neighbour's goods" is a commandment that seems especially appropriate for musicians. It is futile to covet someone else's physical asset such as quick memorizing ability or large hands, and it is well within the realm of possibility to develop your own resources. It is said that the 'cellist Gregor Piatigorsky can learn a whole composition en route in an airplane or train, fixing everything in his mind without even touching his instrument, and play it perfectly on arrival. We who are not so gifted, who must learn the slow, hard, no-short-cut way, can rarely concentrate on more than one thing at a time, but we can work during worktime, play during playtime, and generally find a time and place for everything without living on our bravado, nerve, or accomplishing the seemingly miraculous. Having large hands is not the panacea that so many people think it to be; Rachmaninoff used to complain about his big hands, and Artur Schnabel said that his thick fingers often got in the way. No matter how unfortunate you think your physical pianistic defects are, you can always make the most of overcoming them.

Do not ape and imitate every idea in interpretation you like. Interpretative concepts are very personal; diamonds in one person's hands may be glass splinters in another's. In music mere imitation always sounds synthetic. Only the genuine individual idea, based on a careful study of a score and a composer's personality, is convincing.

Here are two stories that involve the same composition and two opposing viewpoints:

(a) When the pianist Soulima Stravinsky (Igor Stravinsky's son), was living in Paris as a student, he had the great desire to master Liszt's *Feux Follets*. He went to Vladimir Horowitz, who gave him practice suggestions that he followed over a period of time. Apparently still unable to master *Feux Follets,* he returned to Horowitz and was told: "It is within the province of some of us to accomplish certain things at the piano, while others among us just are never capable of mastering certain problems. Don't worry about it; you are a great pianist just the same."

(b) When I was about eleven, I asked Rachmaninoff what he considered the most technically difficult piece written for piano. He deliberated for a few minutes then said: "Well, I suppose that one of the most difficult compositions is the Liszt étude *Feux Follets.*" "I want to play it." "Oh, no, not with your small hands. You could not do it yet." Now I knew I *had* to master it. I set to work and made up crazy, unorthodox fingering, broke passages into two hands, used hand positions that would have made Leschetizky turn in his grave, but I played all the notes and eventually mastered *Feux Follets.*

The point I'm trying to make is that the pianistic problem doesn't exist that cannot be solved by determined imagination. No individual, no book, has all the answers. Many of the most important solutions are in *your* head, *your* heart, *your* hands.

PLATE I

"When you play staccato octaves, such as those in the opening passage of Mendelssohn's *G Minor Concerto*, make your hand into a stiff 'octavo mold', as I call it: the middle fingers curled under so that they will be out of the way.

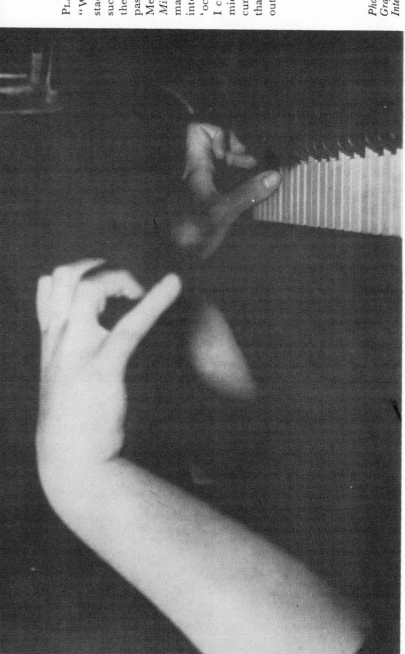

Photo : Servicio Grafico International

★ 5 ★

ABSORPTION AND PROJECTION

A COMPOSITION isn't learned; it is absorbed. It becomes as much a part of you as a finger or a tooth; even better because, along with your mental faculties, it usually improves with age. But before you can absorb a new piece of music, you must be absorbed by it. Your attitude will not be too different from being in love: unconditional fascination, desire to understand weaknesses or roughnesses, willingness to give a great deal of yourelf in order to receive. Mastery of a work of art must be earned. Never be overawed by technical difficulties. A composition may have been written by a musical genius, but even the greatest genius is, first and foremost, a human being, an imaginative human being who wants to share the fruit of his creative upheaval with petty mortals like you and me. It is ours for the taking, with his blessing.

In the preceding chapters I have discussed the problems of proper practicing that apply to the recitalist as well as to the beginner. Even the most accomplished of my colleagues did his first scales at some time in his childhood. As an old Chinese proverb says, even the longest journey starts with a single step.

The first step is to get acquainted with what I call the "musical geography" of a new composition; we have to decide how we want it to sound. Then, I repeat, we play it very slowly, making sure that all the notes and markings are there; we experiment with pedal and fingering, and repeat the easier themes in as accomplished a manner as possible to get them "into our fingers" and sense the general pulse of the melody within the context of the composition. We do this several times a day, meantime proceeding to the difficult passages, subjecting them to the same process. We continue to experiment with the fingering until it feels comfortable. For intricate fingerwork we use the device of accents and rhythms described in the preceding two chapters. We may find it necessary to practice each hand separately, using the metronome, then finally to repeat the whole procedure with both hands together: "developers," rhythms and accents, daily metronome drill. When each difficult passage has been conquered in this manner, we can usually play all the way from beginning to end without stopping and without making mistakes. Even if the tempo is still slow, we are beginning to make music. We put lilt into our themes, we work on the phrasing of our lyrical sections, we begin to *feel* the composition even though we may not yet project it.

However, all these devices should not be used in fugues or polyphonic passages, since they require concentration on many voices simultaneously. I like to mark theme entrances in fugues with colored pencils, to make the eye, as well as the ear, alert to the musical architecture from the start. Artificial accents and rhythms as a learning device here are impossible and confusing.

Actually, I give a daily work session to every composition I have in my current repertoire. It helps me to memorize it, or, rather, not to forget it. A pianist must know his music so thoroughly by heart that he can write it down, accurate to the last detail, at a split second's notice. Daily runs-through are enormous timesavers. Even before we master a composition, little sections will begin to memorize themselves as they become absorbed by our subconscious. First they are like little islands; then some bars before, some bars after, stick in the memory, and together with the transitions whole large sections begin to take shape. Soon, working on the whole composition from beginning to end, from slow to fast, day by day, I gradually find myself turning fewer and fewer pages. Eventually the little islands merge into the whole large entity of the piece, which becomes mine entirely.

At that stage a piece appears to me like a newly born puppy —miraculous and exciting—because, though it quite clearly shows how it will look in the future, it still is clumsy in its spindly, young, inexperienced state. Carefully practising every day, the pianist can concentrate on becoming more pliable, more sensitive to interpretative ideas; he can start to experiment with performance. Until now all his mental and physical faculties were tied closely with taking in; now he has to aim at that state of satiation and abundance where he can give.

Put down the music rack and open your pianoforte to its full extent. You are going to project for the first time. You never heard this composition in quite that way before, and all sorts of new discoveries in the music and in your reaction to it lie ahead. Now, by opening the pianoforte, you are changing one of the listening habits you have formed in practice.

Soon other small habits will change, purely physical habits: I put telephone books on my chair to give myself a different position; then, again, I play the same piece sitting on a low kitchen stool. I have to do something similar all the time on tour. Every pianist has a favourite height for his keyboard, and practically all pianoforte stools are adjustable, but sometimes the exertion of playing a particular pianoforte requires a different body position. Also, the change of seating height helps me to "loosen up," to get a free, unhampered feeling. Singers and violinists who are not glued to their instruments have different methods to get this feeling of physical freedom. Feodor Chaliapin was an impressive, dynamic, giant figure as he strode across his living-room in the Hotel Ansonia, intoning some Russian folk melody. The singers Rosa Ponselle and Elizabeth Rethberg used to walk around their small dressing-rooms at the Opera House, vocalizing before a performance. Violinists Nathan Milstein and Mischa Elman walk up and down as they warm up their fingers. A feeling of space and freedom is imperative for projection.

I occasionally play a new piece unexpectedly, on the spur of the moment, at odd times not on my practice schedule. Each time I listen critically and try to profit from every mistake. Am I making the music say what I intend? I ask an indulgent friend or relative to be my first audience. Then I take the composition out of my home environment; I try it out at a pianoforte store or at a friend's house. This is, in a way, as if my performance would have to earn its wings by experimental flight.

There is the story of a rich old gentleman who decided to take pianoforte lessons, bought a concert grand, and practiced faithfully every day, despite the amusement of his friends and their warning that "you can't teach an old dog new tricks." Once a week the movers would come, take the pianoforte away, and bring it back several hours later. The old gentleman's explanation: "I took it along to my lesson." This story is supposed to be funny, but to me it isn't; many pianists depend on their own instruments and are completely lost when they have to use a different one. Independence from outside factors is a performer's stock in trade.

Here are a few important things to watch for, particularly for the student:

(1) Don't get discouraged during any part of the learning process. "The darkest hour is that before the dawn." Sometimes it may seem to you that for days, perhaps months, you cannot get anywhere with a certain composition, yet you will master it eventually. You may have to give it a rest for a few days. You may have become too closely involved with the composition for clear self-criticism; you may have "over-practiced," grown tense. The chances are that you will be amazed at how well it goes after a brief interval, but, if it doesn't, you were not ready and you'd have had to start all over again, anyway. Just don't give up!

(2) Always have your music handy when you practice so that you can refer to it whenever you have the slightest question. Also, use the most authentic edition you can find and be sure to obey all the markings; thus you will never have to doubt the authority of your performance. If someone offers a suggestion, listen with an open mind, but consult the score before you follow it. (This is not required for fingering and pedalling, however, which are rarely written in by the composer himself; only remember that strong fingers are better than a heavy foot.) Never choose "tradition" over the indications in the original score. Tradition is a much-abused word; Toscanini defined it as "the last bad performance." For his last recording session the maestro studied and restudied the scores he had conducted for decades and the slightest doubt would send him back to the libraries hunting for the original manuscript. Tradition, for him, could be established only by the composer. Never take accepted practice for granted. When a child I played a Beethoven sonata for Wilhelm Backhaus, and he corrected a passage in it, but at home I rejected his correction and practiced it the way I wanted. The next time I played it for him he stopped me. "Mr. Backhaus," I said, "I see it

differently. Why must I play it your way?" His simple reply I shall always remember: "Because that's how Beethoven wrote it."

(3) Be careful not to overaccent, or to place an accent where none was written. Most students go through such a stage and it is perfectly normal while learning a composition. The accents are like road marks that you need badly on strange territory. Once you are more familiar with a road, you may still want to have the map handy, but you no longer have to slow down to read what the road sign says. After you have travelled the road frequently and come to know it well, you won't even notice the markers and will enjoy the scenery. As you play, watch for your little accents and exaggerations, and eliminate them. They won't help you in performance and may damage your interpretation.

(4) Don't exaggerate your teacher's suggestions. When I first played a Chopin waltz for Alfred Cortot, he found my bass notes on the first beat too soft and lacking in rhythmic character. "Your basses have no substance; they don't support the melody. Make your first beats in the left hand at least as firm as this match," he said, and lit a cigarette. At home I tried to make my left-hand first beats, not only in this piece but in everything else I played, as firm as, not a match, but a piano-forte leg. This went on until it was explained to me that (a) exaggeration could lead to distortion and (b) we must not use the same device for different compositions unless it is in character. For example, a Viennese waltz by Strauss will gain by the now traditional lilting hesitation between the second and third beat, but a Chopin waltz would be ruined if played in that manner.

(5) Avoid mannerisms. Theatricals went out of fashion with the silent films, in which gestures had to tell the whole story without the spoken word. At the pianoforte, mannerisms are not only in bad taste but physically impossible except for artists who are not really engrossed in the music. Besides, the natural, effortless abandon that comes with good, relaxed pianoforte technique is sufficiently spectacular in itself.

6

ACQUIRING A REPERTOIRE

PIANOFORTE REPERTOIRE is vast. Most great composers were pianists, choosing the pianoforte rather than a string instrument because the polyphonic nature of the keyboard gives a more satisfying outlet for artistic self-expression. In the old days, before the great masters had composed our repertoires, they had to write their own music when they performed or taught. Bach wrote most of his inventions for his children; Mozart, Beethoven, Chopin, Schumann, Liszt wrote music for themselves or for their students. They wrote it, of course, in a way to make the best of the shape of their hands, their special abilities, their favourite devices. Composing his rhapsodies and operatic paraphrases, Liszt was playing to the public in much the same way as our band leaders do today when they arrange hit songs for their ensembles. He took full advantage of his large hands in writing octave and arpeggio passages, such as in his arrangements of Paganini's Études, which are so difficult that, for many years, no other pianist could play them. Delicate Chopin, on the other hand, gave preference to the type of composition that sounds best in a salon.

In a similar manner the amateur pianist will choose a repertoire that will exploit his best qualities; yet knowledge of pianoforte literature should be well rounded, and a good teacher will always try to arouse a student's curiosity and guide his taste toward a comprehensive repertoire. To fit one's repertoire to one's personality does not mean to take the line of least resistance.

Some professional musicians keep repertoire books in which they make a list of all the compositions they have ever performed, together with dates, places, exact timings, and, if a partner or an orchestra was involved, comments about rehearsals. A professional can't remember everything he has ever studied. The book will remind him of musical experiences and triumphs half forgotten. It is like an inventory; a quick glance will indicate where the repertoire is strong and where it needs to be built up. For the student it is also an excellent progress log, and it is a real morale-booster, when the going gets tough, to see, in black and white, the amount of music already mastered.

Our present tendency toward specialization has also slipped into the concert hall: some artists prefer to play Chopin and other romantics, others specialize in Bach and the early classics, others in Beethoven and Brahms, and there are even some who specialize in contemporary music. I don't think this is good unless a musician's actual repertoire is well balanced and he is able to perform a healthy cross-section of pianoforte literature. Paderewski had a very small repertoire, but it was comprehensive and large enough to make several interesting programs.

When an artist has a well-balanced program, his special fields will stand out in much better perspective. I tell my students to think of general repertoire as the main trunk of a tree; they can explore one branch or another with all its twigs and leaves, but then they should return to the trunk and add what they have learned to strengthen the whole miraculous structure. Later they can explore a different branch, and use the newly acquired knowledge to make the main trunk still stronger. Walter Gieseking, who was famous for his playing of Bach, Mozart, Beethoven, Schumann, and in particular Debussy and Ravel, learned what was for him a completely new musical colour, Rachmaninoff's Piano Concerto No. 2, toward the end of his career, and played it for the first time at the Hollywood Bowl when he was over sixty. Toscanini seldom conducted Tschaikowsky until Horowitz became his son-in-law and persuaded him to accompany him in the Piano Concerto No. 1. The record they made is among the most outstanding, and the maestro was then almost seventy years old.

The two things I caution my students against are arrangements from other instruments, and simplifications of music they cannot play in the original. I also recommend the utmost caution in the choice of sets of variations for a concert program; variations are tiresome for the average listener unless they are short and written by one of the great masters.

Repertoire-building begins at an early age; therefore, the same principles apply to both the amateur and the professional. When it begins—or ought to begin—there will be one youngster in a million who will become a child prodigy, and one in a hundred thousand who can be expected, with a fair amount of certainty, to have a musical career. In repertoire-building the point of departure is the same for the budding Myra Hess as for the home-town girl, whose only audience will be the captive one of family and neighbours.

Very young children of pre-school age may absorb a foreign language more easily than when they are somewhat older, and this also applies to the language of music. Some small children can perform marvels in memorizing quite beyond the comprehension of adults. When I was four, I memorized a Bach invention in half an hour, just before a matinée, and played it as an encore. I would never dream of doing such a thing today.

Some youngsters can learn a sonata in a week, a concerto in two weeks. It takes their elders longer to assimilate, because then we become aware of many other elements to be absorbed with the notes. This may be the reason why so many artists with extensive repertoires were child prodigies who started to accumulate a repertoire when they were very young. When Leopold Godowsky, who was known for his tremendous repertoire, was in his forties, composing, teaching, touring, someone asked him how he found time to learn new things. He replied, "I don't learn them, I know them."

Since the compositions we remember longest are those we have learned during our formative years, the teacher has a particular reponsibility toward the student who wants to become a professional to be sure that each piece of music he learns can become part of a permanent repertoire. For example, a talented pupil will have more opportunity to play Beethoven's Sonata, Opus 27, No. 1, than the "Moonlight", Opus 27, No. 2. It will teach him the same things technically, but if he plays it later in public it will be unhackneyed. It is better for a young musician not to provoke comparisons with the Serkins and Rubinsteins, but to be noted for courage and personality. For the same reason I find it hard to understand why most pedagogues assign Chopin's Ballade No. 1, Scherzo No. 2, Fantaisie-Impromptu, the C♯ minor Valse and the like, when similar, but less familiar works, such as the Ballade No. 2, Scherzo No. 4, Impromptu No. 3, and the F minor Valse would be better investments in terms of learning-time. The pianist will have to learn the better-known repertoire later on, anyway, and he will be able to do so by himself.

There is a definite place for the better-known repertoire in the teacher's studio: with the less talented pupil who is sure that he will never play in public and who studies for the sake of making music rather than for the intangible dream of becoming the world's most famous recitalist. To the teacher whose pupils want to play popular music I say, "Why not?" Use it as reading material to give them the thrill they seek in playing the music in vogue with their set of young friends, teaching them a valuable skill at the same time. The student who cannot absorb much harmony or Bach might still play well enough, and should be encouraged along the lines of short melodious works by Grieg, Mendelssohn, Schumann, Chopin, Mozart, Haydn, Bartók. Many teachers give their students a very good start with the Edwin Hughes Master Series books of unadulterated but easier selections from the great composers.

The teacher should always be on the lookout for good intermediate material that has not been simplified and revised by editors. New collections in all fields of music, including contemporary, are being released on the market constantly, and the teacher should keep posted on all this good learning-literature.

The ideal repertoire-building system for most students seems to be to learn three compositions from different musical periods and of varied styles simultaneously. For instance, the youngster who is practicing a Bach gavotte, a Chopin prelude, and Prokofieff's *Fairy Tale* at the same time enjoys such a pleasant variety of musical fare that he cannot become bored with any aspect of his practicing. The same principle of three contrasting irons in the fire can be maintained at all levels of instruction.

The teacher should have a long-range-potential repertoire plan for each pupil, the details of which can be flexible according to the student's progress. For instance, there is the problem of the student whose present pianoforte ability is undisciplined and showy and who feels that he must play, say, Grieg's Concerto. Now, the pupil probably could be pushed on to this extent, even though most of the passages are beyond him: by trying hard, and with great patience on the parts of teacher, pupil, and the pupil's family who have to hear him practice, he might, at the end of one year, play the first movement through from beginning to end with a lot of wrong notes. It is better to aim toward the Grieg Concerto gradually by mastering a few of Grieg's *Lyrical Pieces,* a couple of Mendelssohn's *Songs without Words,* a Schubert impromptu, a couple of Chopin's preludes and a mazurka, a Scarlatti sonata, a Mozart fantasy, a Kabalevsky sonatina, and finally, at the end of two years, Grieg's entire Concerto, which could have been "softened up" in the student's spare time. It will come easily and sound well because the student has prepared for it properly and has acquired much of the technique of practicing—to say nothing of learning other first-class pleasurable music into the bargain!

It is important to advance a student according to his intellectual and pianistic capacity. For the young student whose hands can't yet span octaves there is plenty of attractive music that doesn't require octaves; such compositions are far superior to simplified versions of the more difficult work that will sound weak in the undeveloped hands and will spell discouragement to the immature mind that does not understand why the piece doesn't "sound right." A pianist with a naturally beautiful tone, but as yet undeveloped power, can play wonderful repertoire, ranging from Frescobaldi and Purcell to Handel, that is completely overlooked by people who delight in exhibiting a powerful technique. A pupil who has good fingers, but whose intellectual power is still latent, can play Weber, Tschaikovsky, Hummel, etc.

The ability to learn is something that grows within a person as long as he keeps this ability active. What a great inspiration was someone like Mischa Elman, who, after fifty glorious years on the platform, kept the youthful musical stamina and vigor to learn new compositions! Arthur Rubinstein, despite his statement that he had no formal lessons after the age of fourteen, learned the most important lesson of all—how to think for himself and let experience be his teacher. Rachmaninoff felt that, as long as one practiced, the hands would remain supple, and continuing to learn keeps the mind young.

Teachers often mourn the loss of a good pupil. This is so unnecessary. Nadia Boulanger described the teaching process as a game of give-and-take. Arnold Schoenberg starts the preface to his *Harmonienlehre* with the words, "My pupils taught me this book," meaning their questions and their mistakes. Teacher and pupil inspire each other with fresh ideas, but they may reach a period of diminishing returns. At this time both gain from seeking fresh fields to grow within themselves and to enrich others. The really great teachers, such as Franz Liszt and Ferruccio Busoni, never had pupils in the ordinary sense of the word, but disciples and friends who played for each other, discussed, and progressed together.

The real musician will be for ever seeking new means of projection, looking over new literature, making up experimental programs. Art has no boundaries and the horizons of accomplishment are always beckoning with new challenges.

7

A PRACTICAL REPERTOIRE LIST

IT WOULD be impossible to offer an ideal repertoire for everybody. While every pianist at every level can benefit by becoming a better reader it is best to select material that is a little less advanced than current learning level. Bach, Handel, Bartok, Haydn are extremely valuable to help strengthen the ability to count correctly. Duets are ideal for this purpose. Chopin's Mazurkas, Mozart's and Haydn's compositions are particularly recommended for phrasing, and for learning to build many small phrases into a large musical line. Bach, Brahms, Debussy make one think at many levels simultaneously and are best used by the advanced student. We recommend all reading to be done without pedal until the hands become proficient in doing all phrasing and legato as marked in the score. We have purposely chosen selections from lesser-known repertoire. Every publisher's new catalogues yield new exciting material in all musical periods and at every level. *Clavier Magazine* features a description of new publications every month. *Piano Quarterly* gives additional useful reviews. It is important to use 20th century music as early in a student's development as possible so that he can develop eye-hand coordination without interference from a diatonically-oriented ear.

In all cases use urtext editions so that the composer's slightest marking can be obeyed. Ignore fingering until you decide to invest time in learning. Then look for patterns and let eye-hand coordination teach you what is best.

E — Easy
M — Moderately difficult
A — Advanced
D — Particularly delightful
T — Especially useful for developing skills in
    techniques

REPERTOIRE FOR THE INTERMEDIATE PIANIST

Composer		*Composition*
Albeniz	DM	Tango D Major
	TDA	Sequidillas
	TDM	La Leyenda
Alexander, Haim	DM	Six Israeli Dances
Anderson, Leroy	DE	Arietta
Auric, Georges	M	Petite Suite
Bach	TDM	(Henle) Praeludium e Fughetti
	TM	Anna Magadalena Buchlein
	TA	Suites (English & French)
	TA	Partitas
	TMA	Inventions
	DM	Italian Concerto
	TA	W.T.C. Books 1 & 2
	DA	Cappriccio on the Departure of a Beloved Brother
	M	Fantasy C minor

Barber	DA	Nocturne
	TA	Excursions
Bartok	DM	Roumanian Christmas Carols
	M	10 Easy Pieces
	M	Bagatelles
	DM	Petite Suite
	TDE	For Children, Books 1 & 2 (Hungarian & Slovakian)
	DM	Rondos on Folk Tunes
	TDM	Sonatina
Beethoven	M	Bagatelles
	DM	Contradanses
	M	Variation Sets
		Irish Folk Song
		Russian Folk Song
		Austrian Folk Song
	TDA	Rondos
	E	11 Viennese Dances
	E	6 Sonatinas (Ricordi)
Ben-Haim, P.	M	Melody + Variations
	M	Sonatina, Op. 38
Berkeley, Lennox	M	Five Short Pieces
	M	Scherzo
Blacher, Boris	M	Sonatinas
Bloch, Ernest	E	Enfantines
Brahms	TDA	Hungarian Dances
	TDM	16 Waltzes

	DM	Ballads Opus 10
	A	Ballad G minor, Opus 118
	TDM	Cappriccio G minor
Britten, Benjamin	M	Night Piece
Brubeck, Dave	DM	Themes from Eurasia
Craxton, Harold	E	A Cuckoo Prelude
	E	The Leaves Be Green
Creston, Paul	DE	5 Little Dances
	M	5 Preludes
Chopin	DTMA	Preludes (Henle, Paderewski, or Kalmus Edition)
	TDMA	Mazurkas
	DMA	Waltzes
	MA	Nocturnes
	TA	Miscellaneous Compositions (Tarantelle, 3 Ecossaises, etc.)
Dello Joio	M	Suite for the Young
Debussy	DM	Danse
	M	Danse Bohemienne
	M	2 Arabesques Preludes
	DE	La Fille aus Cheveux de Lin
	E	Canope
	TDM	Voiles
	M	Danseuses de Delph

	TDM	Cathedral Englouttie
	DM	Bruyéres
	DM	General Lavine, Eccentrique
Dvorak, A	M	Waltzes (Simrok Edition)
Francaix, Jean	M	Scherzo
	DM	Six Grandes Marches
Frarck, C.	DM	Short Piano Pieces
Fuga, S	E	Canzoni per la Gioventu ˎRicordi
Galluppi, B.	EM	4 Sonatas
Gershwin, G.	TDM	Gershwin at the Keyboard
Gianneo, Luis	E	5 Pieces (1938)
	DM	Caminito de Belen
	DE	Music For Children
Ginastera, A.	TDMA	American Preludes
Granados	DM	Spanish Dances, Marks Edition
	DM	Valses Poeticos
	TDM	12 Dances Espanolas
Grieg	DEM	Lyrical Pieces
Guion, David W.	TDM	The Harmonica Player
Gaustavino, Carlos	DM	Gato

Handel	E	Edwin Hughes Book
	M	20 Aylesford Pieces
	A	Suites (Steingraeber or Kalmus Edition)
Hohvaness, Alan	DE	12 Armenian Folk Songs
Harvey Paul	DE	Rumba Toccata
Jazz Collection	M	The Day of Jazz
Khachaturian	DE	Adventures of Ivan
Kodaly, Zoltan	M	Nine Piano Pieces, Op. 3
Kuriaknau, Rena	A	Perpetuum Mobile
La Montaine	DM	Child's Picture Suite (Broude Bros.)
Lavry, Marc	E	Five Country Dances
Lees, Benjamin	M	Kaleidescopes
Liadov	DE	On the Steppes
Liszt	DM	Consolations
Mendelssohn	DM	3 Preludes, Opus 104A
	TDA	3 Etudes, Opus 104B
	M	Song Without Words
Menotti, Gian-Carlo	M	Poemetti
Mignone, Grancisco	DE	7 Pieces for Children
Milhaud	DM	Chansons sans Paroles

	M	Household Muse
	MA	Saudados de Brazil
	E	Touches Blanches
Mompou, Frederic	DM	Scenes d'Enfants
Moore, Douglas	DM	Fiddlin' Joe
	DMA	Suite for Piano (pieces available separately)
	DM	Grievin' Annie
Orff, Carl	E	Kleines Spielbuch
Peters, Florr	DM	10 Bagatelles, Op. 88
Piston	TDA	Passacaglia
Poot, Marcel	M	Six Easy Pieces
Poulenc	M	Pastourelle
	DM	Suite Francaise
	TDM	Presto in B♭
	M	Nonetelle in C Major
Previn, Andre	M	Impressions for Piano
Prokofieff	DA	March from "The Love of Three Oranges"
	DM	Pieces for Children, Opus 65
	TDA	Episodes, Opus 12
	DM	Pieces from "Cinderella"
Rachmaninoff	DM	Italian Polka
	DM	Daisies
	DM	Preludes: G# Minor

	M	G major
	M	F major
	TDA	Oriental Sketch
Ravel	DM	Menuet Antique
	DM	Menuet on the Name of Haydn
	TDA	Valses Nobles and Sentimentales
Rorem, Ned	E	A Quiet Afternoon
Scarlatti	TDM	60 Sonatas (Kirkpatrick)
Schubert	TDE	Samlische Tanze (Henle)
	TDA	Impromptus
	TM	Moments Musicaus
	DM	2 Scherzi
Schumann	TDM	Fantasy Pieces, Opus 12
	TDA	Novellettes
	DM	Papillons
	DM	Scenes from Childhood
	A	Faschingschwark aus Wien
	M	Romances, Opus 28
Shostakovich	M	Spanish Dance
	TM	Album of Selected Works
Starer	M	Five Preludes
	M	Seven Vignettes
	DM	Three Israeli Sketches

Stravinsky, Igor	E	The Five Fingers
Tcherepnin	DM	Songs Without Words
	TM	Bagatelles, Op. 5
Villa-Lobos	DE	Twice Five Pieces
	DA	Baby's Family (Prole do Bebe)
White, Florence +Akiyama, Kazuo	DE	Children's Songs from Japan
Willert-Orff, Gertrud	DE	Kleine Klavierstucke

DUETS

Bacon	E	Hootnanny
Bartok	DM	Pieces and Suites
Bizet	M	Children's Games
Bruchner	E	3 Little Pieces for Piano Duets
Debussy	DA	Petite Suite
	A	6 Epigraphs Antiques
Dello Joio	DE	Family Album
Diabelli	E	Pleasures of Youth
Handel	DM	Suite From The Water Music
Hohvaness	DE	Child in the Garden

Milhaud	DM	Suite Francaise
Moskowski	A	Spanish Dances
Mozart	M	Original Pieces
Poulenc	DA	Sonata
Rachmaninoff	DA	Italian Polka
Ravel	DM	Ma Mere l'Oye
Rozin	E	Two Together
Schubert	M	Original Pieces
Schumann	DA	Original Pieces
Stravinsky	E	5 Easy Pieces
Tschaikowsky	DM	50 Russian Folk Songs
Villa Lobos	DM	The Little Train of the Caipira
Zeitlin & Goldberger	DM	11 Piano Duets by the Masters

8

BUILDING A CONCERT PROGRAM

PROGRAM-BUILDING is a difficult art and should never be attempted hastily or casually. There are different kinds of programs, each with its own intrinsic laws.

A full recital, meaning a varied concert program, should present examples of the various composers' finest music. It will naturally show the performer at his best. It should be a healthy mixture of familiar and less familiar music, including at least one modern composer to convey the feeling that music is a contemporary, living thing.

Short-group programs have an entirely different basis. Here the pianist has no more than fifteen minutes to show his ability to best advantage. To me the best formula is to use a bright opening number, then a contrasting slow work (but not too slow in order not to break the momentum of the group) and a brilliant finale demonstrating technical prowess. Have a bright encore ready. And play only whole compositions; excerpts or single movements from sonatas or suites have no place on the programs of a serious artist.

There is also the one-composer program, all-Beethoven, all-Chopin, all-Schumann, for example. The performer has to be careful to present a varied picture, a good, bird's-eye view of the composer's works: some of the strongest and most famous; some lesser-known ones; and others that illustrate

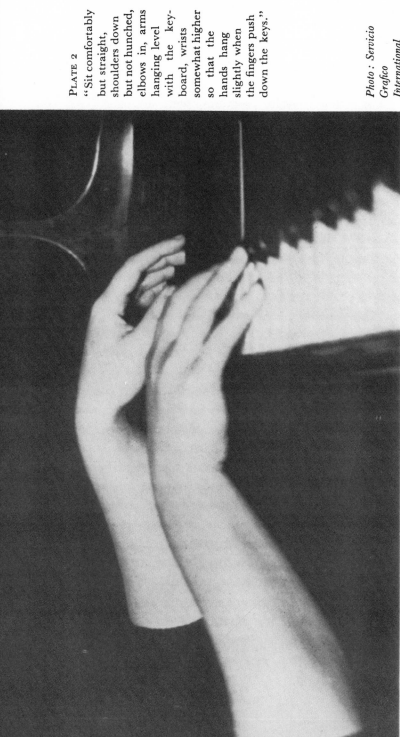

PLATE 2

"Sit comfortably but straight, shoulders down but not hunched, elbows in, arms hanging level with the keyboard, wrists somewhat higher so that the hands hang slightly when the fingers push down the keys."

Photo : Servicio Grafico International

particular characteristics and subtleties. In other words, it should be a well-rounded, comprehensive musical portrait of the man.

For a time "novelty programs" were in vogue. They consisted only of toccatas, or études, or preludes, etc., and had a certain educational value: they illustrated how different composers treated the same type of composition.

Like every fashion, that of program-building is in a constant state of flux. Every ten years we have different heroes, villains, and whipping-boys. One season there will be a "run" on Schumann's *Carnival* or the Liszt sonata, or Beethoven's "Appassionata," and for some seasons thereafter these works will take an enforced vacation, only to be revived again by a number of performers simultaneously.

For the person who is interested in the historical development of concert programs, the big libraries have fascinating material on the nature of successful ones in, say, the days of the Bach family. In the good old times a concert was a big social event, the talk of the town until the next concert. It often lasted for many hours, well into dawn, and included excerpts from solo sonatas, chamber music, symphonies, arias sung by leading singers; with assisting artists often borrowed from variety shows—acrobats, magicians, jugglers. Beethoven once conducted a concert in which, between movements of one of his major works, a violinist demonstrated that he could play with his instrument held upside down. Improvisation on the pianoforte was a major item; Mozart, Beethoven, Liszt were famous for their improvising even before they reached fame as composers. Often the theme would be a popular tune or current hit chosen by the audience. Otherwise almost everything was played from the music until the virtuoso days of Thalberg and Liszt, who revolutionized recital practice. When Clara Schumann, as a prodigy of twelve, returned to

Germany from a tour and played by heart after the example of these two men, whom she had heard in Paris, she was severely criticized for her "unmusical desire to attract attention by circus tricks."

Liszt presented the first solo pianoforte concerts and, showman that he was, he sat so that the audience could see his handsome profile; formerly they always saw the performer's back. I firmly believe that only by learning about the past can we see the present in its proper perspective and dare participate in future developments. Liszt rightly said that Father Time was the most authentic music critic.

Wherever we live, whether in a hamlet or a metropolis, we are influenced by the cultural climate of the area. It is human nature to believe that local newspapers write the worthiest and most important opinions, that the local orchestra and its conductor occupy the most respected positions in the musical world, that our local music-teachers dominate the area's musical thinking. When we travel and visit a larger city, perhaps another continent, we begin to get a truer picture. Since it is hard for most people to travel much, perhaps the best method of keeping *au courant* with cultural events and styles is to subscribe to the most important paper of a musical metropolis, and keep a scrapbook of programs and reviews to follow the development of young talent; to watch, over a period of time, the trends in program-making as they are molded by critics and public opinion. Why not make a hobby of studying young artists, their programs and reviews, their training background, their potential, and of trying to predict who will be the immortal of tomorrow? The history of the world is documented by cultural trends; it is fascinating to watch the relationship between world news and cultural achievements.

Working with the artist and repertoire producers at my

recording company has taught me an important lesson in program-building: that there need be no hard-and-fast rule of order in the list of compositions on a record. The same is true for a recital. For a quarter of a century we used to place music chronologically; to start with Scarlatti or Bach, proceed through the romantic period, delve into a modern or contemporary group, and end with a grand finale, usually a tried-and-true war horse, to bring down the house. Thousands of successful programs have been built along these lines. In fact it may be the adherence to this format that brings about the statement, every once in a while, that this generation will hear the last piano recital. So much good music is available on records and radio that audiences don't have to leave their comfortable living-rooms unless enticed by an extraordinary event. But I still believe that an interesting program, carefully and tastefully built for variety, color, substance, and novelty, can get the most tired businessman out of his armchair and into the concert hall.

Ideally, your program should last about seventy minutes. Your first number should not be too long, so that the incorrigible late-comers don't have to feel that they are not getting their money's worth. I like a good and strong start because it puts the audience into an expectant frame of mind; also it should avoid displaying your full case of fireworks, so that the mood of your program can grow in excitement. First choose your *pièce de résistance* and build around it: a masterwork like a sonata by Beethoven, Schumann, or Mozart; a Debussy suite; a Bach partita; any major work from any musical period. If you want to use two masterworks, choose contrasting ones from different musical periods and of different architecture—not two sonatas, two suites, etc., but preferably a sonata and a suite, or a set of variations. Also, if you have a very tuneful work, *don't* follow with another just as tuneful; your audience won't remember either melody; nor arrange similar rhythms to follow each other, such as two waltzes, or a waltz and a mazurka. To play a dramatic work just before intermission is excellent policy; as in the theatre, it will create suspense. Then, after the intermission, you may play one of your long selections; people are rested and ready to give you their close attention. Don't have two compositions of the same genre unless you deliberately want to point up contrasting styles: for example, select a waltz by Schubert and a waltz by Chopin; but you may play a prelude and fugue by Bach and a prelude and fugue by Shostakovich. Sometimes it is very effective to have two contrasting compositions in the same key or relative key—a nocturne and an étude perhaps—to succeed each other; this is like placing a light blue flower next to a dark-blue, one enhancing the other's shade. When you have several short compositions, don't play them in a monotonous row, such as slow-fast-slow-fast; better use a variety of musical shades, such as soft and sad, quick fingers, melodious and dramatic, brilliant fireworks. Get as many different moods into your program as possible. Place your soft, slow pieces to best advantage when the public needs a rest from something dramatic. Don't let your program lag on the penultimate number; use a fast nocturne or a slow waltz, or a catchy light melody; your program must keep its sweeping momentum. Let your encores be a continuation of your program in quality and in added colors. If you have a favorite composition that you, in a way, identify with personal experience, make it your last encore always, like a signature at the bottom of a painting.

Audiences in different parts of the world require different programs. Germans have a long musical tradition and like a heavier program of pure music with at least two major works that will challenge their intellect. The Gallic and Latin audiences prefer to be entertained with a majority of lighter compositions. The English, Dutch, and Scandinavians are slow to express their reactions, but they are extremely alert and intelligent listeners who require a carefully balanced program of abstract and contemporary works. In general, European audiences are very sophisticated. The Brazilians and Argentines have made a national hero of Chopin. For South Americans concerts by internationally known artists are major events and they have exacting ideas of performance, shaped by constant listening to recordings of the world's greatest soloists. They expect performers to have an individual, identifiable style; more than anywhere else, performers are judged on the basis of pure ability, plus the way in which they play Chopin.

Frequently professionals judge the quality of young début artists by the originality and care that go into the building of their programs. Even for an experienced performer it takes a long time—sometimes weeks of concentrated thought, effort, and research—to assemble a program on which they will stake their reputation for a concert season.

Let us now analyze several representative concert programs:

PROGRAM BY VLADIMIR HOROWITZ

Sonata in Eb major	Haydn
Two Songs without Words:	Mendelssohn
May Time	
Shepherd's Complaint	
Pictures at an Exhibition	Moussorgsky

INTERVAL

Impromptu in Ab major	Chopin
Nocturne in F♯ major	Chopin
Ballade in G minor	Chopin

Serenade to a Doll	Debussy
Étude for Four Fingers	Debussy
Toccata, Opus 11	Prokofieff

Analysis

The central feature is Moussorgsky's *Pictures*. Notice the variety in mood from the beginning to the end of the program; never once is a color repeated.

The Haydn is a classic, pristine, yet bright opening. The two contrasting Mendelssohn songs whet the listeners' appetite for the monumental romantic Moussorgsky suite.

The Interval gives the public a rest, and the familiar Chopin compositions afterwards will not tax their stamina. The two contrasting Debussy pieces are both a balance for the two Mendelssohn songs heard earlier and a relief between the lyricism of Chopin and the steely brilliance of Prokofieff.

Possible criticism

The main work, *Pictures*, was not the original composition but Horowitz's arrangement; there is so much fine pianoforte music available that arrangements can easily be avoided.

PROGRAM BY ARTUR RUBINSTEIN

Chaconne	Bach-Busoni
Sonata in E♭ Opus 81 a ("Les Adieux")	Beethoven
Intermezzo in B♭ minor, Opus 117, No. 2	Brahms
Capriccio in B minor, Opus 76, No. 2	Brahms
Rhapsody in E♭ major, Opus 119, No. 4	Brahms

INTERVAL

Polka, "The Golden Age"	Shostakovich
Vision Fugitive, Opus 22	Prokofieff
Suggestion Diabolique, Opus 4, No. 4	Prokofieff
Barcarolle, Opus 60	Chopin

| Nocturne in C♯ minor, Opus 27, No. 1 | Chopin |
| Polonaise in A♭ major, Opus 61 | Chopin |

Analysis

For color, variety of rhythm, pace, mood this program is exemplary. Rubinstein, knowing how wary of contemporary music an audience can be, wisely places Shostakovich and Prokofieff before the Chopin group, which he uses as a great crescendo and climax. Notice his use of unhackneyed Chopin.

Possible criticism

This program is too full of sure-fire, smaller, familiar pieces. It might be improved by playing the entire cycle of Brahms Opus 119, which ends with the Rhapsody, instead of using the Intermezzo and Capriccio from different groups. The cycle is a complete suite with the same continuity as a sonata, and it would add weight to the program without making it longer. It would also improve the balance, for there are only short pieces after the Interval.

Shostakovich and Prokofieff are similar in character; it would be better to contrast styles, using, for instance, Bartók, Poulenc, or Barber instead of Shostakovich.

The idea of playing a Bach transcription is open to criticism among purists who argue that, inasmuch as Bach wrote so much keyboard music, it is not necessary to play a transcription from the violin.

PROGRAM BY DAME MYRA HESS

Rondo in D major, K. 485	Mozart
Adagio in B minor, K. 540	Mozart
Little Gigue in G major, K. 574	Mozart
Sonata in A major, Opus 120	Schubert

Partita No. 1	Bach
Sonata in C minor, Opus 111	Beethoven

Analysis

Here is an artist who uses the classics with imagination in building an interesting and charmingly tuneful program. The Mozart Adagio and Gigue and the A major Schubert sonata are seldom heard and have the effect of important re-discoveries in the hands of a master.

Notice the beautiful program-balance: three short light classics before the romantic long Schubert; then, after the Interval, the more familiar dance movements of Bach's classic Partita, leading to the last Beethoven sonata, a dramatic crescendo of magnificent music.

Program by Walter Gieseking

Partita in B♭ major	Bach
Three Sonatas	Scarlatti
Fantaisie in C major, Opus 17	Schumann

INTERVAL

Barcarolle, Opus 60	Chopin
Pagodas	Debussy
Reflets dans l'Eau	Debussy
Rhapsody No. 9	Liszt

Analysis

This unusual program is admirably balanced. The artist wisely builds toward the focal composition, Schumann's Fantaisie, to draw attention to the new romantic colours. He builds a crescendo up to Interval and then starts a decrescendo with Chopin, to reach the quietest possible mood with *Reflets*. Finally, the Liszt Rhapsody brings the audience to their feet in a roaring climax.

At the same time Gieseking gives similar balance to each half of the program by including the short sonatas by Scarlatti, which represent different intensities of the same classic shading, to counterbalance the short pieces by Debussy, whose impressionistic, ethereal pianoforte sound is his speciality.

ALL-SCHUMANN PROGRAM BY JOSEF LHÉVINNE

Études Symphoniques, Opus 13
Toccata, Opus 7
Four Pieces from Fantasiestuecke, Opus 12

INTERVAL

Carnival, Opus 9

Analysis

This is a magnificent program, which includes the two most famous works of Schumann, the *Etudes,* and *Carnival.* Only captiousness would insist that one of the lesser-known sonatas should be substituted for one of these major works. The artist's interpretation of the hair-raising Toccata was one of the technical feats that made him famous; the introspective *Fantasiestuecke* makes the Schumann color palette complete. Notice the perfect balance in placing a long major work at the beginning, and another one after Interval, when listeners usually are at their most receptive.

Caprice on the Departure of a beloved Brother	Bach
Sonata in B♭, Opus 106 ("Hammerklavier")	Beethoven

INTERVAL

12 Études, Opus 25	Chopin

Analysis

This program cannot fail. It is centered around the titanic "Hammerklavier" sonata, a work so difficult to carry off well that only half a dozen pianists in each generation succeed. The Bach is a light, charming introduction. After the interval comes a big surprise for Serkin fans: the second book of Chopin études is a major pianistic feat, outside the territory of this artist who specializes in the German-Austrian school.

Possible criticism

A short lyrical piece of more recent music, perhaps Prokofieff, Bartók, or Ginastera, between the interval and Chopin, would supply additional color.

PROGRAM BY RUTH SLENCZYNSKA

Sonata in D major, Opus 10, No. 3	Beethoven
Excursions	Barber
Ballade No. 2, in F major	Chopin
Étude, Opus 10, No. 1	Chopin

INTERVAL

Carnival	Schumann
Italian Polka	Rachmaninoff
Hungarian Rhapsody No. 15	Liszt

This program was built around two contrasting works: an early classic, the Beethoven sonata, and the romantic *Carnival*.

The juxtaposition of the sonata and the contemporary, almost jazzy American suite forms an interesting background for the two Chopin works.

The spectacular étude, with its broad sweep, placed before the interval, uplifts the audience who will have to concentrate on the long *Carnival*.

Rachmaninoff's unfamiliar Italian Polka is light, short, and tunefully dainty between the long, rich *Carnival* and the fervent brilliance of Liszt's rhapsody.

Possible criticism

The four-movement Beethoven sonata is quite long for an opening number. If a shorter sonata had been chosen, there might have been room for a complete, short, softly lyrical composition to round out better the variety of the program; the best place for such a melodic work would have been just before or just after the *Carnival*.

Present trends indicate more concern with 20th Century composers. Bartok, Barber, Prokofieff, Shostakovich no longer excite curiosity. They are replacing Liszt, Mendelssohn, Grieg, St. Saens. We are eagerly auditioning oracles of the future.

9

PREPARING A PROGRAM

PREPARING a program has every much the same aspects as preparing a fine meal. There is a deadline; there is a variety of different tasks to perform, and they all have to be at their peak at the same time.

For my personal schedule I advance the deadline by about six weeks, if possible. (Artists who travel almost all the year round have to prepare much of their program en route; it is difficult, but it can be done.) A six-week margin usually leaves me some time to rest and to polish my program so that I am completely ready when concert time arrives.

It is possible to establish some sort of work schedule if you know approximately how much time you can give yourself every day. Four hours, preferably divided into two periods of two hours each, are a bare minimum. Each person's working capacity has a different rhythm, closely related to our physical condition, basic metabolism, body temperature. I see no point in fighting against it if you don't have to; you'll need your self-discipline for other aspects of your work. I'd rather suggest that you organize your work accordingly and rotate your material so that you get the maximum return out of the time invested. Many people are at their best after breakfast and at their worst after lunch, and they wake up again when everybody else wants to go to dinner, which is very inconvenient but cannot be helped. I am a "night person" and my best times are early morning and late at night; my ideal daily practice schedule is three periods of two and a half hours each.

I warm up slowly; it takes me at least an hour of practice before I hit my learning-stride. It is a difficult job—and I sometimes wonder whether any of us really likes to work—but the challenge is fascinating. Before a concert we all bemoan our miserable lives; afterwards we wouldn't change places with anyone else in the world.

No one is at his peak all the time. On some days our minds will be more alert; on others our best practice will be at the functional muscular level; a third time our interpretative powers seem to have special inspiration. When we rotate our practice material, we can take special advantage of these bright periods. Much of the time, dull days are a symptom of our reluctance to getting started. With a variety of different material on which to work we are sure to be fascinated by some aspect of the practice routine if we give it half a chance. Sigmund Freud said that laziness is simply fear of not succeeding; I have found that consistency of effort at least prevents total failure, even if the spark of inspiration eludes us temporarily.

Once we have definitely selected our program, we should start with the most difficult parts of it and begin to soften them up. I take the most intricate single composition to be learned and play it every day from beginning to end. I do this first thing during the morning period and spend at least one hour working it over to become closely familiar with it. Sometimes I spend the whole morning practicing this difficult new piece without even noticing the passing of time. This is good. I reserve at least half an hour, possibly an hour, of my evening practice, just before I stop for the day, for reviewing and smoothing down the same work.

If I am very tired after the morning's first hour, I start practicing on the most routine technical thing on the program. This gives my learning-apparatus a rest while I exercise my fingers on material I will need. Metronome slow-to-fast practice is particularly good here because the forced steadiness has a calming effect and you have the comfort of resting mentally and accomplishing something at the same time.

Next, I suggest listing all the routine passages and starting with the most difficult one. As the days go by, the "most difficult" will come under control and you can be satisfied just to review it and proceed to the next problem, and so on down the line. The first hour of afternoon practice can be spent softening up the next-to-most-difficult new composition; the remainder of the afternoon session should repeat the morning's metronome practice. In the evening, depending on how tired you are, either start by softening up New Work No. 2 or repeat metronome practice for the third time. Always end a working day by a strong review of the most difficult new work.

This is Phase No. 1, the "ugly duckling" stage we all go through when we haven't a thing ready to play except maintenance repertoire we have in hand without special practice. It is good for an emergency, but not gratifying to play when preoccupied with new and exciting material.

As we put most of our time into Composition No. 1, learning it as described before, part of it will eventually reach the finished stage. We put the finished parts aside for the time being and concentrate on the stubborn section. When we have conquered these, we forget the whole work for a while and promote ourselves to No. 2. We finish this and replace it by No. 3, etc. As we proceed we eventually find that we have covered the whole program and whatever encores we have in mind—three are the ideal number.

Now comes Phase No. 2: divide the whole program and encores into three parts from beginning to end. If you have three practice periods, spend the first two hours of each on playing through one program-part at a time, just as if you were playing the concert. Get into the spirit of each phrase of every note. Let yourself go. If you feel like creating a particular effect, check with the music and go overboard if it is permissible. Probably you will exaggerate, but that is exactly what you want to do at this point; it is like going over every detail with a magnifying glass to make sure that you are playing correctly. By repeating the whole program day after day you will start to think in terms of the program unit instead of the composition-unit. If you are a great pianist you will also develop a characteristic sound so that the music can be identified, just as a connoisseur can identify a painting by the brush-strokes.

The remaining half-hour of each period will be spent in slow-to-fast metronome practice of all the difficult passages in the program. Now we are overlearning, building up a margin of reserve. We are building each passage to a speed beyond that which we will need. We are practicing chord passages, using our strength from slow-to-fast so that when performance calls for power we have a comfortable reserve under control.

Gradually, by dint of repetition, the exaggeration will file down, the rubati assume shape and control, extremes in dynamics and tempo will be softened, and the individual subtleties of each composer and each composition will come through, not glaringly, like headlights on a highway, but like the topography of a vast and varied landscape as seen from an airplane. The end of Phase No. 2 never comes; we advance for ever.

Artur Schnabel had a detailed master-plan for everything he played. He even had words to each phrase of a Schubert impromptu or a Mozart sonata. I find this a bit extreme, because I prefer to "interpret" by letting the music speak for itself; yet this was Schnabel's way of making every note fit into place. It is very important to have some general and detailed plan in mind. There are times when inspiration does not come as freely as usual; others when our instrument does not co-operate satisfactorily. I know a 'cellist who has several alternate plans of approach for every major composition on his programs, which he uses according to the weather, that is, its effect on his Stradivarius. So, even when, for some reason, we are not at our best, we can still have a solid and good performance as long as we have an architectural master-plan as a lifesaver.

Now we can take a little rest, a weekend at least, completely away from music. From here on, the program is yours and you've earned it. You've bought it with devotion and work and honesty to the composers. But you don't own it completely until you can give it away freely, with confidence and assurance. You must play often and be ready to play everywhere.

In *Life* magazine I saw a picture of neophyte paratroopers playing ball while they were strapped to fifty-foot poles. The caption explained that the trainees were, at first, dazzled by the height and were afraid to trust their safety belts, clinging to the poles with both arms. Playing ball, throwing it from one pole to the other, the boys had to use at least one arm, eventually both arms to throw, and so became accustomed to the feeling of height and learned to trust their safety belts. Your careful practice is your safety belt.

There is always room at the top for a great artist. There can never be enough beauty. There always are too few great personalities. The line that separates the "very good" from the "great" is slim; it is crossed by that extra effort of performance, that extra grain of imagination, that extra feeling of rapport with the audience, that extra warmth of humanity that pervades the artist's personality. With work, courage, imagination, honesty, it is within your power to enter that magic land of creative beauty. The late architect Frank Lloyd Wright said that luxury is far more important to man than necessity. We should think in terms of glamorous sound, voluptuous tone, dazzling technique, and be satisfied with nothing less. If you think on the grand scale, you will produce accordingly.

People who come to the greenroom ask me many questions. One is, "How can you play well when you have to maintain such a heavy concert schedule?" I answer that it is easier to play a season of fifty concerts than one of ten because you constantly build physical and mental stamina. It is most difficult to play only one concert a year. Constant performance keeps the polish at a high gloss and, as in baseball, continuous training gives you a high batting average. "What happens when you are not in the mood to play?" is another question. This always startles me. There can't be such a possibility. An artist does not perform by caprice. His function is to *create* a mood, a whole atmosphere for himself and his audience. Practicing makes an artist so sure-fingered that, even on off-days, his performance will have quality and scope, and he will be able to reach his public. I firmly believe that temperament is 90 per cent temper—that is, bad manners—and 10 per cent fear. Use the awareness of your consistent effort and the margin of reserve you have acquired to fight actively the demon of fear. If we allow it to enter our thoughts, we can be afraid to play a single piece, a small passage, even a single note. With fear it is simply a question of degree. What is the worst possible thing that can happen if you make a mistake? Your loss of reputation? Then, don't seasoned professionals who have great reputations have far greater cause for fear? Absolute perfection in art is impossible because everyone's concept is different. Who can be the judge? Whose concept is the right one? "Don't you ever make a mistake?" mothers of young pianists often ask me. Well sometimes. We all do. No matter how hard we have worked and how well prepared we are, the public's excitement sets all the senses keenly aware and we listen and project differently from any other time. Surprising things happen, mostly caused by nerves. When you feel that you have made a slight mistake you are terrified ; you lose all sense of proportion. Suddenly your memory blacks out; you clutch blindly at any straw of improvisation that will take you back to the beginning, or skip to the end or the nearest break or theme that you can remember in your frenzy. The whole thing lasts only a split second, and it feels horrible, but if we have practiced hard enough to have a high batting average it may not happen again for the next fifty concerts.

Making mistakes is almost inevitable at some stage of absorbing a certain work. I don't know of any great pianist who would not occasionally slip, and even the one I think is least liable to make mistakes is not beyond a wrong note once in a while. This is not to encourage carelessness or a casual attitude toward accuracy; we must strive for maximum perfection. Yet, since we cannot skip the stage in which absorption of a work is not yet completed, since we have to go through this period of comparative instability, I wish that so many young artists were not so completely disheartened and frustrated when it happens to them. One of my colleagues— whom I consider a superb musician—is, in my opinion, handicapped in a big career only by his overanxiousness to give a flawless performance, which takes much of his spontaneous musicianship away.

Fear of critics should be no issue in performance. A critic so alert and erudite that he notices every slight slip will, by the same token, be a superior musician who will see it in proper proportion and make no issue of it if the rest of the performance is an accomplished, professional job, serious, convincing.

ABOUT LISTENING

To LISTEN is, according to Webster, "to give an ear" or, according to Funk & Wagnall, "to heed what is heard." Listening is meaningful and conscious hearing, a special art that must be cultivated. There are many different ways in which people listen to a piece of music:

1. Most people, I believe, are first of all fascinated by the performance, and I have heard remarks like, "did you ever see hands move so quickly?" or comments on the "fine left hand" or "brilliant octaves."

2. Other people are primarily entranced with the effect of the music. They don't pretend to know much about the technical part of playing; they have no ambitions for themselves; they go to a concert purely because they like music. They look for certain clues in the program to know what they can expect: sounds reminiscent of rippling water in a composition called *The Brook*; the association with gypsy fiddles, firelight, and dancing in Liszt's Hungarian rhapsodies. These are the people who say that they don't know music but do know what they like, and a concert either leaves them cold or carries them away completely.

3. Yet some people will compare a performance to other performances they have heard. This is almost inevitable with older people, who tend to be nostalgic for their own youthful

receptiveness, and it always happens with people who have had a strong "first impression" of a composition and establish it as a yardstick.

These individual methods have limitations, however, and those limitations spell certain dangers. The ideal way to listen has something of each of them.

Intelligent listening is an art that any layman can cultivate by directing his conscious attention to all the clues: production, effect, instrumental sound, and "comparison yardstick."

Music's message reaches people in devious ways: it can appeal primarily to the emotions, or to the senses, or to the intellect. Music can change a person's mood, but the person has to be pliable and willing to co-operate. When you go to a party you can have a boring time if you sit back and do nothing, or you can have a marvellous time if you pitch in and help to create for yourself, and those around you, a festive spirit. The honest listener must, first of all, learn to respond.

If we could ask Beethoven or Bach how their music should sound, we would probably be greatly surprised at their answers. Those masters did not have our instruments and could hear their music only under conditions that would not satisfy us nowadays. Sometimes, too, composers are less qualified than re-creative artists in the art of interpretation. When I played one of his works for Heitor Villa-Lobos shortly before his death, he made several suggestions which I immediately carried out. Then he said, "No, play it the way you feel it, the way you think it should be done."

We all have musical concepts which we develop in imagination. We identify ourselves with the performers whose ideas are bigger and better-developed versions of our own. (That is the principle on which synagogue cantors have always been chosen; their songful prayers are supposed to be the idealized embodiment of the prayers of the whole congregation.)

Those of us who are mainly interested in technique will identify themselves with a great technician whose clarity and brilliance are foremost in evidence. Those who want to be carried away by the music, regardless of production, will find their ideal in performers who re-create musical splendor, perhaps with a slight disregard for perfection.

The most important thing is to be open-minded to every kind of music. As in flying, there are invisible barriers. It was a tremendously difficult task to break the sonic barrier because it involved concepts in physics, in methods of flying, in forces never experienced. Most people have similar hidden barriers in their minds; we call them prejudices. They are man-made walls; they exist in our minds because we put them there and are very reluctant to take them down. Barriers were erected against Palestrina and Bach, against Brahms, Wagner Debussy, Strauss, Bartók, Stravinsky—against practically any innovator.

Another mental barrier is the preconceived idea. Some people have the notion that all Mozart must sound delicate like a pink china doll, that all Brahms must sound heavy, that all modern music is discordant. When we hear a performance that doesn't agree with our preconceived ideas we become critical, nonplussed.

How many people go to a concert and wait to read the reviews the next morning to see whether they enjoyed it! How wrong! Musical taste is a very personal thing. Often you can be guided by other people's qualified judgment and stimulated to investigate further, to sharpen and educate your own feelings, but you have the last word in matters of personal preference. The greatest hope of the re-creative artist is that his study has been so thorough, his concept so honest and convincing, that he will epitomize the concepts of most of his listeners. As an audience, we should make a special effort to develop our own tastes and opinions, and not disclaim them. It takes a great deal of receptive listening to reach the sophisticated state where *only*, say, chamber music, or contemporary music, or English madrigals, or some such special field, can satisfy a person's musical taste; in fact, when I meet such a person, I question his sincerity. First, one must try everything, from Purcell to Puccini, from Bach to Bartók. We must listen to men's choruses and harp solos, to E. Power Biggs and Vladimir Horowitz, taking in everything with an open mind. When you like something, listen to it again. There is no such thing as "good" music or "bad" music. The most popular music is that which was acclaimed by listeners who unashamedly formed their own choice. Beethoven is good box office today because people for one and a half centuries have enjoyed his music enough to want to come back for more. Regardless of whether, in your musical taste, you become a conformist or non-conformist, a faddist, or a conservative, be candid. There is the Hans Christian Andersen story about the emperor's new clothes that supposedly only the very wise could see, until a child innocently pointed and said, "Look! The emperor has no clothes on at all!"

Choose honestly the things you like best, enjoy them, learn about them and their composers, analyze them from the viewpoint of performance and its effect on you, and be proud of developing your own good individual taste. You can have a lot of fun by turning on the radio and trying to identify the music that happens to be playing. There are plenty of musical clues. First try to identify the period: is it classic, romantic, impressionist, contemporary? Does it have themes or rhythms that seem indigenous to a particular country? Do the melodic or harmonic styles remind you of another composer's works? See how close you can come by guessing.

You will find that, as you develop into an analytical listener and discover new sound colors, your musical taste will become broader and different. If you don't like Bartok today, give him another chance next week, next month, next year. Human nature is afraid of the unfamiliar, and most great masters had to run the gauntlet of hesitancy, criticism, even hostility. One of Mozart's string quintets was returned by a publisher who felt that the copyist must have made a mistake; Mozart couldn't possibly write such dissonances. Wagner had to build his own theatre to realize his ambitions and was almost sixty before he was acclaimed. Beethoven was patted on the shoulder by some critics and told to improve his style by listening to the music of some third-rate *salon* composer. Richard Strauss and Stravinsky provoked riots in the concert hall. It is impossible to know whose music will be heard in a hundred years and whose will be forgotten. But we can, and should, champion our choice of today. The false fear of saying the wrong thing makes many of us with valid and authoritative opinions retreat to platitudes and generalities. What is the point in being merely tolerant? No one, and certainly not an artist, wants to be merely tolerated. Artists need encouragement, acceptance, constructive criticism.

The words "mature" and "immature" are being abused to a degree that invites discussion. Webster's dictionary defines "immature" as "unripe, not arrived at full development". A fruit slowly ripens in the sun all the spring to achieve a brief period of maturity; then, if not picked, it becomes overripe, deteriorates, and spoils. The work of an artist mellows, develops, and matures all through his life. Full maturity would imply perfection, the peak, but as we perfect ourselves we constantly discover new areas to explore. An artist's whole life span is taken up with the maturing process; in this sense, he can never hope to reach absolute maturity.

Not every artist, however, will admit this fact. It takes a

certain amount of humility. One of the humblest people I have ever met is Mischa Elman, despite the many stories that circulate about his vanity. Once a gushing lady addressed him in the greenroom and swooned: "Mr. Elman, you are a god." Elman, sharp-witted as always, replied: "No, madam; a god doesn't improve, but I do."

In art, as in life, the Why and the How are often more significant than the What. If we try to understand why a certain artist deviated from the traditional pattern, and if his playing can convince us from his point of view, then we might just as well accept it on its own terms even though we disagree.

The vast American public stayed away in droves from Rubinstein and Gieseking when they were in their artistic prime. Rachmaninoff and Harold Bauer knew the bitterness of critical condemnation. Think of how many more years we and they could have brought enjoyment to each other had we but listened to their art instead of waiting until a lifetime of hard work earned them sufficient reputation to bring forth the applauding public. Let's not make the same old mistake over and over again; let's not wait for artistic merit to find us. By developing our own musical taste and having confidence in our own judgment we can rejoice in our own discoveries and champion the artists of today, the proud heritage of tomorrow.

★ II ★

FROM MY TEACHING EXPERIENCE

MUSIC CAN be taken up at any time. A good teacher will use as many different approaches to instruction as he has students, for no two individuals are alike. A grandmother can find tremendous pleasure in studying the piano (it is healthy for her fingers, too). A businessman will find piano practice a great nerve-soother and will get a real thrill of accomplishment from producing attractive melodies through his own efforts. The slogan of the Orchestre Symphonique de Paris is: "One can live without music but not as well!"

If a child grows up in a home where music is a part of everyday living, he will subconsciously develop a broad musical taste even before he ever attends a concert. He does not have to sit in reverence during an entire radio or record player reproduction of a classic; enjoying music should not be irksome, but a pleasure. When the child attends his first live performance it will be a revelation to him to watch music "come to life."

The most important things a music teacher can give to a student are a healthy and realistic attitude toward music, good pianoforte habits, a feeling of security at the keyboard, and the ability to sight-read pleasurably. With these assets the student can look forward to reaching musical independence; he will be able to come back to his music at any time and go on without a teacher if need be. If he manages also to acquire the ability to play "show pieces," they should be regarded as dividends rather than the net result of his music lessons.

The main thing is that the beginner has faith in his teacher and stays with him only if he trusts him implicitly. Studies in the psychology of learning show us that if we plot learning ability on a graph it will be shaped like a giant S—periods of progress will alternate with plateau periods that will seem comparatively fallow. During such periods we will need confidence in our teacher and in our objectives.

Teachers can help a student enormously by writing down the next lesson's assignment and telling him clearly what his daily preparation for that goal should be. For instance:

Play C-major, A-minor, G-major, and E-minor scales and arpeggios both hands together, with the metronome at sixty, at four notes to the beat.

Read a Burgmüller study *carefully* every day.

Learn the first section of the assigned Bach invention by playing it six times with each hand every day, paying special attention to phrase and dynamic markings. Lift hands for rests.

Play a Schubert waltz, as if in a concert, twice at the end of each practice period.

Review Bartók dance. Make an exercise of the mordents in the right hand.

Read Chapter No.—— from Ethel Peyser's *How Music Grew*.

This indicates clearly what the pupil is expected to accomplish in his practice period. It reminds him of important points that might slip his mind. Also, over a period of time, parents, teacher, the pupil himself, can follow his development and see which material was covered and which practice methods were used. Clara Schumann's father, who was her teacher, made her keep a musical diary, which she kept nearly as long as she lived. Many youngsters who "don't want to practice" really don't know *what* to practice or how. Parents can co-operate by monitoring the work from time to time, offering praise and encouragement, and assigning a definite unalterable period every day as Practice Time. An hour per day is the absolute minimum that cannot be replaced by, say, a three-hour session twice a week. The mechanics of playing require the physical drill of constant repetition. A well-planned and well-balanced study program will give optimum results even with a pupil of limited time and talent. The child will accept this discipline and enjoy it, even though he may occasionally grumble—as we all do sometimes at everyday tasks.

Further, to accustom the student to communicating the music he has learned, the good teacher holds informal class meetings periodically—about once a month—where students can listen to each other, discuss repertoire, and enjoy the experience of performance. For special occasions, such as a composer's birthday, students could be encouraged to practice a particular segment of their repertoire; how about a Beethoven Festival, or an Evening of Contemporary Music? A book report by at least one pupil on a teacher-selected music book should be read at each gathering; perhaps a prize could be given to the best report on the assigned book. Artists constantly learn new works to fill new programs; pupils do the same, even if their "concerts" are only in the teacher's studio. Artists' performances improve with every concert; teachers should create opportunities for all their pupils to perform as often as possible. Theodor Leschetizky used to invite all his pupils to bring their music on an appointed evening; the music was placed on a table and the master selected one piece at random that was played by the student who had brought it. A conscientious teacher will find many ways to stimulate a pupil.

POSTURE AND HAND POSITION

Begin by learning good habits at the keyboard. The easiest way is often the best; relaxation and alertness are necessary to all physical effort. Sit comfortably but straight, shoulders down but not hunched, elbows in, arms hanging level with the keyboard, wrists somewhat higher so that the hands hang slightly when the fingers push down the keys. One of my earliest teachers, a Leschetizky pupil, called this high-wrist position a "Roman Arch." (See plate 2). This suspension of the hand from the wrist causes the tone to be controlled by the weight given to each individual finger when pressing down the key. This weight touch gives us relaxed control in all finger technique and production of tone. Solid, firm fingers are the foundation of a good finger technique; each finger must be well raised and firmly put down so that every key touches the bottom. Sit with your backbone ramrod-straight. When you play at either end of the keyboard your whole body moves in that direction so that the body's strength can support the hands. Anton Rubinstein obtained his famous power by leaning the whole trunk of his body forward, backbone still ramrod-straight, to add its weight to a chord. Artur Schnabel used to lean back to give the hands a floating feeling during a cantilena phrase.

LEARNING NOTES AND RHYTHM

A very young beginner can learn to find C by establishing that it is immediately to the left of the two black keys. He can make a game of finding C all the way up and down the keyboard. Then he finds CD, CDE, and we are off to a good start in learning the names of all the white keys. To teach the concept of sharps and flats, explain that the smallest possible interval on the piano is called a semi-tone. A semi-tone to the right, whether the key is white or black, takes the name "sharp." A semi-tone to the left, whether the key is white or black, takes the name "flat." The same process takes place with the concepts of a tone. In this way the beginner gets an accurate and healthy way of thinking about sharps and flats on the pianoforte, and also an introduction to rudimentary harmony through his early familiarity with intervals.

COUNTING

When the beginner learns to count, help him to understand the digits as a horizontal reading concept rather than a variation of arithmetic lessons that the child associates with vertical lines. Use "and" freely—"1 and 2 and 3 and 4 and . . ." For triplets say "1-and-and, 2-and-and, 3-and-and, 4-and-and." For semi-quavers say "1-i-an-i, 2-i-an-i, 3-i-an-i, 4-i-an-i." Dotted notes will not be a problem if the teacher writes the proper counting numerals and syllables from left to right on the student's music until he understands the new concept. While the pupil is perfecting this new skill, he should count every new piece through, away from the keyboard, until he can hear the composition correctly with his inner ear.

SOLFÈGE

In Europe solfège, the art of verbalizing music, was considered for centuries an essential part of every student's training. It is presumed to be an invaluable aid in reading and memorizing. It takes quite a bit of practice to become adept at saying out loud all the Italian syllables (do, re, mi, etc.) to the notes of a Bach prelude up to speed. The underlying purpose of getting the music into your consciousness is a good one. It seems to me, however, that many of the best solfège students become so mechanical in this skill that it loses its value, and I merely suggest it as an extra aid when necessary. For example, in learning an intricate finger passage the fingers may learn more rapidly than the brain, and the memory may fail to retain every note; in such a case the student will mentally review the problem and use solfège to learn more thoroughly. One colleague checks memory by reviewing a whole composition using one finger and playing one note at a time.

HARMONY

The study of elementary harmony is of vital importance to every talented music student. The mind and the ear must recognize intervals, both melodically and harmonically. Harmony will also teach someone who has "no ear for music" to recognize the basic mathematical laws of symmetry that are the skeleton of all composition. If a student has learned the basic harmonic pattern of a major scale and can transpose it in his mind as well as with his fingers, he will not balk at reading compositions containing a number of sharps and flats in the signature. The study of harmony will get the mind accustomed to directing the fingers at all times; using the inner ear, the mind will memorize harmonically, and that knowledge will enable us to form a clearer mental picture of the composition's architecture. The study of harmony is a lifetime's necessity. After the student acquires a basic introductory knowledge, he and his teacher can decide whether to continue and take up counterpoint and composition. Just as the study of Latin is valuable to the specialist in languages, elementary harmony is an essential part of a gifted pianist's early training. The teacher can choose from many available manuals the method that proceeds according to the needs of the individual student, and assign lessons that he can absorb most easily.

SCALES AND ARPEGGIOS

It takes years to acquire real hand-familiarity with the keyboard. During this time there should be daily practice sessions featuring a definitely planned program of scales. Most of the music of Western civilization is built from the basic tones of one or several of the twenty-four major and minor scales. To have a complete hand-knowledge of them is essential, and a sensible investment for future freedom from technical fear. The standard best fingerings for major, minor, chromatic scales, and arpeggios have long since been established, and these fingerings seem most comfortable for all hands, regardless of size. The imaginative teacher will find stimulating ways in which to make scales and arpeggios interesting. Some technical material should be practiced as routine as the warm-up during every study period. The muscles become loosened and accustomed to the movements and will function automatically when the need arises. Dexterity that can be taken for granted is the most valuable tool of which musical imagination can make use. It means freedom. So often nervousness, or a pianoforte's light action, or just plain exuberance will cause us to take an unusually fast tempo that will tax our powers of concentration to the limit. We have to know that our hands are trained so that we can rely on them to carry the passage, whatever the circumstances.

Scales and arpeggios in all the major and minor keys, and the chromatic scale in four octaves up and down the keyboard, are an absolute necessity. We are not going to write them all out here because it is easy to acquire a manual that lists them all correctly and with good fingering. The teacher and student can have a lot of fun devising ways of practicing these essentials:

Hands separately.

Hands together at intervals of a third, sixth, octave, or tenth.

Cross hands (both ways), particularly useful in promoting independent action of both hands playing together.

Staccato (finger, wrist, from the elbow).

Forte in one hand, piano in the other.

Legato in one hand, staccato in the other.

Different accents, as indicated on p. 36.

With the metronome slow to fast.

Both harmonic and melodic minor scales should be studied in all the tonalities. Dominant-seventh arpeggios in all positions are extremely useful to develop the fourth fingers. Establish new harmonic sequences every day: C to D flat, etc. C to F, etc. C to G, etc.

Examples:

C major, C minor, dominant seventh starting on C (CE♭ G♭ A♭), leading to D♭ major, and so on, until you complete the circle.

C major, C minor, dominant seventh starting on D (D F♯ A C), leading to G major, and so on, until you complete the circle.

C major, C minor, dominant seventh starting on C (G E G B♭), leading to F major, and so on, until you complete the cycle.

To make up good sequences is good practice.

Two problems often beset the beginner learning the scales and arpeggios: (1) moving the thumb under the hand quickly and smoothly, without moving elbow and arm; (2) moving the hand over the thumb without jerking the elbow.

Here are some ways to avoid these mistakes: blocking scales and arpeggios.

Examples of a "blocked" scale and arpeggio. Let your thumb do all the work!

Solving the "thumb-underneath" problem is of particular importance, and if you don't seem to need special exercise at first, you may need it later when you work with the metronome to acquire speed. Keep your shoulders down.

FINGERING

Here is our favourite fingering for the chromatic scale:

ascending C to C, right hand 2313123123412

left hand 1313214321321

descending, right hand 2143213213132

left hand 1231234123131

We suggest this because the 1 2 3 4 gives added smoothness in speed by giving the thumb a rest. We don't recommend the two-octave chromatic scale fingering that seemingly follows the same smoothness and rest-the-thumb principle, because it accustoms the hand to a two-octave sequence, and most chromatic scales in compositions are not so long. The one-octave sequence is simpler for the hand to memorize, and more practical. It is also important to learn the chromatic scale in the three back fingers, particularly in the right hand, but also in the left.

ascending C to C, right hand 5343453434345

left hand 4343543434354

descending, right hand 5434343543435

left hand 4534343453434

When your right hand is ready for the chromatic scale in minor thirds, here is the best fingering, derived from Busoni:

ascending, thumb on C 3453434345343

1212212121221

descending, 2nd finger on C 3435434343543

2121212212122

This is applicable to major thirds and fourths as well. The sliding second finger ensures a smooth legato line, both ascending and descending, A chromatic scale in thirds is not easy to master. It is a veritable hurdle, takes a long time and a lot of patience, but it is a proud accomplishment. Use every device: developers, accented rhythms, metronome slow to fast.

As I have a small hand, I find that the best fingering for

chromatic scales in sixths and octaves is the combination of the three back fingers, as above, and jumping thumb. It may be that a larger hand will find something more suitable. In any case, turn your wrists toward your body so that your hands are pointed in the right direction.

Fingering is a very personal matter: what is best for one pianist need not necessarily be best for another. The important thing is for every pianist to have basic, automatic fingering patterns that will be the solid foundation of a sure finger technique. The only way to establish them is to be consistent during practice sessions. Only in this way can we be sure of our kinesthetic response. If perchance during a performance, some minute accident occurs that "derails" the fingers temporarily, the mind will bring the hands back to their whole pattern immediately. Having a fingering pattern firmly established in the first place is the best insurance against being "derailed;" moreover, if the pattern habit is established firmly enough, it will take very strong jarring to upset kinesthetic response.

SIGHT READING

Learning to become a good reader can be a simple, most enjoyable occupation. You should always improve reading technique; even concert artists continue to work on it. It is imperative right from the start to learn to read without looking at the keyboard, similar to the touch system in typing. For the early beginner I recommend Burgmuller studies, Bertini etudes, Schubert Waltzes, miniature pieces by Grieg, Handel, Mozart, Purcell. Duet reading material is particularly helpful in developing a good sense of rhythm. It is important to become free of ear dependency. Small pieces such as Bartok's Hungarian Peasant Songs, Rumanian Christmas Carols, or Prokofieff's "Cinderella" Suite or Visions Gigitives promote eye-hand coordination. Eventually, reading something every day, the student should go through all Scarlatti, Haydn, and Mozart sonatas, the Haydn and Mozart symphonies (in four-hand arrangement), Handel sonatas for violin and piano, etc. The literature is infinite, and curiosity is the best guide.

Learn early that music is a thrilling group activity. To be an accompanist is a special art and teaches you team-work. Accompany a chorus or string ensemble, solo violin, vocal selections from light operas, and you will learn to blend and mould your own tone. Play chamber music and try to inspire your partners with beautiful sound and rhythmic pulse. It is also the best preparation for concertos. The experience of co-operation, of melodic and rhythmic rapport with other musicians, of listening to others as well as yourself, of making adjustments and allowances while keeping up your own responsibilities—all of the many elements in piano-orchestra relations can be learned in chamber music in a most pleasurable way.

Reading well means to read *everything in the score*. Reading is the first step in learning a new composition and it is of paramount importance to read so completely that no mistake will be learned. Correct notes and rhythm, rests, tempo and dynamic markings, legato slurs and phrasing; the ability to keep the eyes ahead of the hands, of noticing scale and arpeggio patterns so that fingering will be smooth: all these skills can only be perfected by the daily reading of music throughout your musical life.

12

SILENT KEYBOARD PRACTICE

SILENT practice is the act of complete performance at a normal pianoforte keyboard without sounding the keys. The fingers play on the key surfaces only, the inner ear hears what the results should be, the emotional impact of the music is rehearsed internally, the muscles go through all the motions of playing; the touch is controlled so that there is no sound. The intelligent use of silent practice can greatly develop dependable tactile response, one of the most important assets of a good pianist. Pianoforte playing involves the whole physical being, all the senses. Silent practice throws, as it were, a spotlight on the tactile sense so that we can consciously develop it to improve performance.

Many talented musicians reach a point where their minds and inner ears hear their ideal of how they want a composition to sound, yet are physically unable to reach this ideal. Practice is the only solution, but it is so painfully repetitious that it dulls the sensitive ear and sometimes closes the enquiring mind. Arthur Rubinstein tells us that in his early learning years he sat at the piano with a good novel and a box of chocolates to sweeten the onerous labour! While theoretically accepting Poor Richard's precept that "diligence is the mother of good luck," many serious students find themselves trapped in a hopeless circle: "I can't play because I won't practice; I can't practice because the repetition will drive me mad." Silent practice will exercise the fingers, and engage the thinking mind without abusing the musical ear. Past generations of pianists thought so highly of developing tactile response that silent keyboards were especially manufactured to be their inseparable companions on tour. I travel with a silent no-action keyboard of 88 keys and have used it for hours of practice in hotel rooms and airports as well as backstage as a warm-up device before performances.

Eager pianists want, and have a right to expect, important repertoire that is always ready for performance. Too many young artists turn down playing opportunities because they are not prepared. This is mistaken prudence; timidity and self-consciousness can only be overcome by successful performance. It would be far better and more practical to strengthen the kinesthetic reflexes so that compositions will be thoroughly worked through, and will remain in presentable condition, and require less time and effort to recall. Silent practice contributes to this mental luxury. A silent hour each night and early morning with the metronome to control speed and with the score to check mistakes will cause the fingers literally to "own" a composition. The mind will be free to concentrate on musical content while tactile response will provide a reserve of accuracy and speed that will sparkle!

Silent practice is especially useful in emergencies where no other type of practice is possible. How often young artists have complained, "My pianoforte is so bad; it won't stay in tune and the keys stick." Or "The only time I have to practice is at night or very early morning and my neighbors want to sleep." On concert tour, due to publicity commitments, often my only free time is after midnight, and my only practice pianoforte a sorry over-worked upright in a closed hotel bar. At home, if I want to lead a normal social life, I must depend on odd practice hours. Even when no emergency exists it is a good idea to give the ears a rest during normal practice sessions. While exercising the fingers, concentrate on glamorous sound, develop your expressive ideal, and magically, through internal preparation, your hands will obey you with new control.

Many kinds of pianoforte problems can be partially solved or aided without sound; reading and getting the fingers accustomed to a complex new composition, hours of slow-to-fast metronome drill on a difficult toccata, complete review of major concerto. Silent practice attunes the inner ear to listen more carefully, to crave for the sound that is deliberately withheld. Later, when normal performance is resumed, the ear will be even more sensitive; fresh beautiful sound will afford delightful release.

Memorizing will be substantially shortened through the supplementary use of silent practice. An important partner of the aural and visual senses, tactile development will train finger patterns to become subconscious so that they will be able to take over if necessary during a memory lapse—an enormous comfort to all who play in public. The kinesthetic aspect of playing the pianoforte is very much like the actor going through a role without costume, scenery, or properties; he depends on his inner knowledge rather than on a variety of outer stimuli. Without pitch or timbre to distract, weaknesses can be discovered and corrected. Greater responsibility is placed on the inner ear, the active hands, the internal musical experience; new depth is brought to performance.

Silent practice is of special value when re-learning a composition because the review is accomplished with a minimum of harsh repetition. The mind is fresh to concentrate on long line, control of dynamics and tempi and search for emotional sustenance.

"Talent is work," said Maxim Gorki. But equally true are

the words of the Queen Grandmother Elizabeth of the Belgians: "Talent is authority." The ambitious musician makes the most of every opportunity to perfect his art.

13

THE USE OF THE TAPE-RECORDER

THE use of the tape-recorder helps to establish the habit of objective listening, supplements as a memory aid, and can be used as an orchestra at one's elbow for concerto and chamber music learning; it can monitor progress, stretch the student's mental horizon, and bridge the gulf between mere knowledge and actual accomplishment. While many of us are familiar with the tape-recorder's uses, a full résumé of its potential services merits our consideration.

It is a complex procedure to learn a new composition. The mind is filled with necessary production problems; the eyes, ears, and hands are completely occupied and one is too occupied to listen. A taped performance, carefully followed with the score, will bring to attention myriad details of structure, tone colour, and rhythm, even before it is played up to speed. To the conscientious listener the taped performance stimulates objective criticism : Is the performance communicative? Does the melodic line flow smoothly? Is the balance of lyrical and dramatic material in proper porportion? Are the rhythms properly integrated? Is there continuous playing momentum? The tape-recorder trains the ear to be alert to correction and improvement, and encourages the mind to test fresh ideas. The simple fact that the composition comes from a source other than from one's own instrument makes one listen more objectively and focus attention on the performance rather than on one's self.

The person who uses the tape-recorder as a memory aid will be delighted with the results. He can tape a slow-to-fast metronomed practice session, making sure that it is free of mistakes.

This tape can be played softly at all times accompanying all kinds of activity; such as writing, eating, cleaning house, sewing, even sleeping; until every note of the composition is assimilated. Take care to make a fresh tape every week so that it will absorb only the most developed performances. Repetition breaks through the outer shell of our mind to our sub-conscious. The anatomy of memory includes aural, visual, and kinesthetic mastery; by deliberately strengthening any one of these elements, we improve the quality of the whole memory procedure. By constant repetition, the tape-recorder will instill aural responses imperceptibly, pleasurably, accurately. Visual and kinesthetic responses can be mastered through silent practice.

I was once asked to play a concerto which I had never studied before. I found the engagement so tempting that I took the challenge of preparing the difficult work at very short notice. I would not have been able to feel confident of a good performance had I not used the tape-recorder as described.

One of the causes of memory failure during the stress of performance is that the mind must make hundreds of decisions per minute about notes, pedalling, tone color, rhythm, harmony; the tape-recorder impresses accurate decisions into the mind so that correct responses can be expected sooner and with far greater security. According to an old English proverb, "God gave us memory so that we can enjoy roses in December." The luxury of comportable memorization can spell the difference as it were between owning the composition for ever, or its total loss. Even years later a thoroughly memorized composition can be recalled in a few hours. On the foundation of accurate memory, the whole interpretation and eventual mastery of the composition will grow.

When studying a concerto, the intelligent student can record the orchestral accompaniment on a pianoforte and "play with orchestra" at will as soon as the solo part is learned. Where a record is available the orchestral tuttis can be re-recorded on tape from the disc to be a constant setting for the soloist. A great deal of the drama, the unaccustomed excitement of playing with full orchestra, can be imported to the learner's studio so that experience can be gained in privacy. Unhappily most artists get only one orchestral rehearsal which is hopelessly inadequate for the neophyte who is facing a whole series of "firsts." Aural preparation by the tape-recorder smoothes the way so that the over-whelming thrill of a full collaboration with the orchestra will be anticipated.

The budding artist has many additional uses for the tape-recorder. After all the composer's score markings are obeyed, the young interpreter enters the realm of communicative and evocative performance which can only be achieved in relation to his maturity and experience. Everyone who practises regularly knows that suddenly there will be a day when the accumulated effort will cause a performance to glow with greater warmth and freedom. Use the tape-recorder to capture these moods. Analyze and identify the physical action responsible for sustaining the spell. This is how to extend self-knowledge and control of the instrument. Spontaneous moods will reveal many different methods of projection, all of which can be stored for future use.

The concert performer has the added responsibility of having only one opportunity to cast his spell; all his knowledge and preparation must be revealed at an appointed time and place when it must come forth brilliantly, convincingly. The student at every level should be encouraged to prepare a weekly program for the tape-recorder and should regard this as a real concert. At a given time the tape-recorder should be set and the program played—for better or for worse. The results should be followed with the scores, for correction, evaluation, and comparison with other tapes for week-to-week improvement. It is one simple thing to form an aural image of the composition, but quite another to make the performance speak with authority and conviction at a certain time. A very talented young woman I know was constantly frustrated in her efforts to play at her best before a panel of judges. Weekly performances of her program for the tape-recorder would have raised her average and eliminated her uncertainties. A person needs practice in playing, as well as practice in practicing.

Natural pitfalls, such as the tendency to exaggerate tempi and dynamics, indulgences in musical clichés, are easily corrected at the learning stage. Professionals play often, and try to improve with each concert, so that their average is a highly practiced production with sparkle and finish. Preparation for an examination or a student recital can start with simulated concerts many months in advance. Results, not efforts, are the judged standard. The weekly tapes file a case history of gradual progress.

After the original purchase of the recording machine, tape is quite inexpensive. It can be used over many times. Tape will erase bad samples or retain progress charts. The microphone should be placed approximately where the hearers would be seated so that it becomes habitual to aim sound towards the audience. This sound in fact is quite different from that heard when there is too much preoccupation with performance. It is deliberate eavesdropping. Work with this finished sound, strange as it may seem, until it is molded and controlled. Impartially, simply, honestly, arrive at musical truth. Compare the interpretations of seasoned artists. One should experiment and arrive at one's own successful solutions. Professional sportsmen use slow-motion films to analyse and improve their ability in much the same way. It is the artist's duty to take full advantage of every tool at his command; it is his privilege to shape, as well as to reflect, his epoch.

At a recent ballet rehearsal I heard George Balanchine give directions to his dancers that might well serve as an inspiration to us all. "Heads up; look high! The floor will always be there." The tape-recorder helps us to achieve performances nearer to the heights of our heart-felt standards.

14

CHART OF ORNAMENTS

THIS CHART includes the most common ornaments to be found in key board music of the Classic period; the illustrations are applicable to composers of the 17th, 18th, and early 19th centuries.

The main change that occurs at about the time that Beethoven was composing his last Sonatas is that   or frequently would have an indication to start on the main note; gradually this indication was left out and the predominant usage became to start on the main note rather than on the upper auxiliary. In the 17th and 18th centuries, symbols were a kind of shorthand to indicate embellishments that were complicated to write; realization of these symbols called for spontaneous imagination cultivated by the playing experience and good taste of the performer. Sometimes these embellishments were carried to excess and many composers including Rameau and J. S. Bach wrote down examples for usage.

Reading draws attention to areas of agreement and disagreement among specialists in musical research. As a practical performer I have tried to include those signs on which most authorities agree.

For the interested student I can heartily recommend:

C. P. E. Bach, *True Art of Playing Keyboard Instruments*, New York, 1949

Putnam Aldrich, *Ornamentation of J. S. Bach's Organ Works*, New York, 1950

Walter Emery, *Bach's Ornaments*, London, 1953

Erwin Bodky, *The Interpretation of Bach's Keyboard Works*, Harvard, 1960

Edward Dannreuther, *Musical Ornamentation*, London, 1893

Ralph Kirkpatrick, *Domenico Scarlatti*, Princeton, 1953

Manfred Bukofzer, *Music in the Baroque Era*, New York, 1947

♪♪♪♪

Ornaments

⋏⋎	**Short Mordent**

Played:

Lower note is auxiliary.

Ex: *Bach* Invention 5 in E♭major

opening measure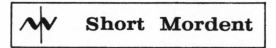

Played:

Ex: *Bach* Italian Concerto, Second Movement

bar 4
right hand entrance

Played:

———————— ♪♪♪♪ ————————

∿ Long Mordent

or

Played:

Lower note is auxiliary.

Used mainly in Handel's keyboard works, it is fully described in C.P.E. Bach's "Essay on the True Art of Playing Clavichord" (Leipzig, 1780).

Note that length of ornament is adjusted to note value. A longer note gets a longer ornament.

Ex: *Handel* Suite No. 1 in A minor

opening bass note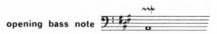

Played:

Ex: *Handel* Suite No. 1 in A major, Gigue

first bar

Played:

For a similar symbol with different interpretation, see Nachschlag.

———————  ———————

tr **Trillo** or **Inverted Mordent**

or

Upper note is auxiliary

tr is a synonym for ᴧ or ∿∿
It can be followed by a nachschlag
or not. The performer can try all
the possibilities and let good taste
be his guide. In the "Table of Ornaments" that J.S. Bach wrote as a
guide for his nine-year-old son,
Wilhelm Friedemann, he gives a
six-note figure for the trillo:

Played:

These are a lot of notes for a value
of less than a quarter, such as an
eighth or sixteenth note, and so, as
in the long mordent we suggest
for shorter note value.

Played:

In rapid finger passages the trillo can
be abbreviated further to become the

Snap or Schneller

Played:

Therefore the symbol 🎵 can mean:

1

on a note value of ♩ or more.

Ex: *Bach* French Suite No. 5 in G major, Bourrée

beginning in right hand

Played:

penultimate bar

Played:

2

on a note value of ♪ or less than a
quarter.

Ex: *Bach* Partita No. 1 in B♭ major, Praeludium

Played:

Ex: Sarabande of B♭ major Partita

bar 4, first quarter

Played:

bar 8, fourth quarter

Played:

3

in a rapid passage of eighths or
sixteenths.

Ex: *Scarlatti* (Longo 241) Sonata in A minor

bar 5

Played:

Ex: *Scarlatti* (Longo 416) Sonata in D minor

bar 24

Played:

Tempo and skill have created their
own tradition:

Ex: *Beethoven* Sonata Op. 13

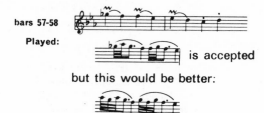

bars 57-58

Played:

is accepted

but this would be better:

Delayed Ornament

Occurs in a lyrical passage when the note which precedes the ornament is identical to the upper auxiliary.

Ex: *Bach* French Suite No. 5 in G major, Sarabande

bar 3

Played:

Note that C (eighth note) is identical to C which is the first note of the trillo. Repetition of the C would break the legato line; therefore it is tied and the ornament is delayed.

bar 32

Played:

bar 28

Played:

𝆖 or 〜〜   Continued Trill
or 〜〜〜   (Shake or Tremolo)

Starts on upper auxiliary and frequently has a suffix (see Nachschlag), particularly when used in a cadence. Because of the nature of

the instrument (the tone of a harp-
sichord cannot be modified by
finger pressure and the sound
vibration is extremely short) the
trill was a device for making a note
sound for a longer interval. Further, in order to simulate a crescendo, a skilled harpsichordist
would measure the notes of his
trill, starting with fewer notes,

etc.

and increasing the tremolo at the
end. On the piano, a trill is still
a good device for keeping a melody
note sounding over several bars,
but because a crescendo is easily
accomplished, measuring the notes
is unnecessary if the tremolo is
evenly and quickly performed.

Ex: *Bach*   Invention 7 in E minor

bars 7-9

Played:

or, with
Nachschlag

Ex: *Bach* Praeludium XVI in G minor

last half measure

Played:

or , with
Nachschlag

Notice delaying tie in order to avoid repetition of C.

A continued trill ought to be even
rather than fast; it ought not to give
the effect of being measured, yet
for practice purposes measuring
is a helpful device until greater
freedom can be established.

Ex: *Mozart*   Cadenza to Concerto in A major (K.488)

bars 26-29

Played:

etc.

Later, after much slow-to-fast
metronome practice, strict measuring can be abandoned in favor of
a free trill. The same is true in the
following:

Ex: *Beethoven* Sonata Op. 53, Rondo

bars 55-61

∿ **Turn** sometimes ∿

Generally starts on upper auxiliary in Baroque or Classic music. When accidentals other than those in the regular key signature are intended, there is a special indication in the score. Context plays an important role in the rhythmic use of the turn.

Ex: *Haydn* Sonata in C major No 32 (chronological order), First Movement

bars 20-25

P ayed:

bars 29-31

P'nyed:

Ex: *Mozart* Rondo in A minor (K.511)

bar 7

Played:

In actual performance, up to speed, it sounds like

bar 10

Played:

or

Within the context of a dotted
eighth and sixteenth melodic figure,
the turn has a special rhythmic pattern.

Ex: *Mozart* Rondo in A minor

bar 17, second half

Played:

bar 30

Played:

Ex: *Mozart* Sonata in F major (K.332), Adagio

bar 1, second quarter

Played:

Compound Sign

This sign is synonymous with short
∿ with nachschlag.

Ex: *Beethoven* Sonata in F major Op. 54

bar 18, third quarter

Played:

bar 24, first quarter

Played:

 Short Appoggiatura

Written with line, the small note is
played almost together with the
main note and let go immediately.

Ex: *Bach* Praeludium IV from W.T.C. Bk. 1

bar 2

Played:

 **long Appoggiatura**

Without line, the small note is played on the beat and is given at least
half, sometimes full note value,
which in turn is subtracted from
the main note.

Ex: *Bach* French Suite No. 5, Sarabande

bar 2

Played:

——————————— ———————————

 Slides

Abbreviation for slow appoggiatura.

Ex: *Bach*   Sinfonia 5

last measure

Played:

Prefix or **Vorschlag**

Usually two notes leading up to trill, trillo, or other ornament.

Ex: *Bach* Italian Concerto, Second Movement

bar 26, last quarter

Played:

 Usually a turn ∾ that starts on upper auxiliary and precedes trill or other ornament.

Ex: same composition

bar 16, last quarter

Played:

 ∿ can function as appoggiatura.

Ex: *Bach* Sinfonia 5

bar 12, third quarter

Played:

⌇ **Suffix** or **Nachschlag**

Usually a two-note ending of a trill
consisting of a lower auxiliary and
main note. Often the nachschlag
is written out in notes so that the
symbol is unnecessary. The nachschlag is especially effective in the
setting of a cadence and at the end
of long trills.

Ex: *Bach*   Partita No. 1, Sarabande

bar 2, first quarter

Played:

More than any other embellish-
ment, the nachschlag can be cultivated by the performer's imagination.

Ex: *Bach* Fuga VI from W.T.C. Bk. 1

bar 2, third quarter

Played:

Ex. of Vorschlag and Nachschlag:

Bach Praeludium XI from W.T.C. Bk. 1

Played:

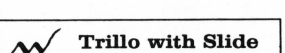

the trill should be unmeasured

--- ♪♪♪♪ ---

∿ Trillo with Slide

Used less frequently than other
ornaments, it serves the purpose
of moving gradually from one
melody note to a distant one.

Ex: *Bach* French Overture, Gavotte II

bar 3

Played:

bar 7

Played:

‍ᴧᴠ can also be contracted.

Ex: *Bach*   Fughetta in C minor

bar 26, second
and third quarters

Played:

‍♪♪♪♪

(( ) [[ ]   **Parentheses**

Usually an abbreviation for a mordent. This sign is frequently found in French composers such as Rameau, Couperin, etc. The same sign can also indicate a long appoggiatura. The performer should use his own good taste as a guide and in the case of parenthesis can omit the ornament entirely should he prefer the music that way. The style of old French music, however, calls for more, rather than less, ornamentation.

Played:

Auxiliary notes should always conform to the basic tonal pattern of the passage in which the ornament occurs. In a modulating passage it is effective, according to some authorities (including Nadia Boulanger), to anticipate the new key, even in opposition to an accidental occurring in another voice.

Ex: *Bach*   Italian Concerto

bar 112

Played:

right hand E♭ conforms to G minor, which is confirmed at bar 115, although left hand is playing E natural

15

CLASS TEACHING AT THE COLLEGE LEVEL

TODAY'S AVERAGE student pianist has an urgent need for proficiency in music reading skill supplemented by dependable finger pattern technique. At college age a young musician usually reaches toward (a) performing major musical works, (b) conquering technical hurdles found in these works, and (c) exploring literature that will make increasing demands on his versatility and ingenuity. Few people are sufficiently good sight-readers to make a musical evaluation or derive pleasure from an introductory reading of material one notch above their actual playing ability.

Too often students get their sight-reading from painstaking "picking" and quickly memorizing their assigned compositions, and spend their time polishing these pieces rather than on acquiring sight-reading as a useful skill. Usually left to develop by chance (bless choral and band directors who draft high school piano students as accompanists!) sight-reading is frequently the factor that holds and sharpens the musician's taste and molds aural concept. What happens to the ninety-nine out of a hundred others who are often equally gifted and potentially sensitive musicians? The habit of poor reading with too-quick, faulty memorizing causes frustration that curtails musical exploration, growth, and enjoyable performance.

Music reading is a necessary, easy-to-acquire skill that, once developed, will remain at a high level and improve with use. Along with a general review of scales, arpeggios, and other common technical problems, music reading is smoothly acquired in a classroom situation. The private lesson is then free to be devoted to repertoire, musical values, details of fingering, phrasing, pedaling. Fingering is largely determined by the size and shape of the pianist's hand, phrasing detail beyond the written direction is shaped by the artist's musical concept, good pedaling should be governed by the sound which is unique to each performer on each instrument. This area comes under the heading of interpretation and is decidedly private; from here will come artistry. Reading and finger pattern technique are public; these should be common tools which form the basis of solid piano playing without which there can be no artistry.

Sight-reading includes varied components: (1) ability of the hands to find their way accurately around the keyboard without assistance from the eyes which should read ahead, (2) ability to see simultaneously and accurately the notes, note values, touch markings (legato, staccato, detached, portamento), phrase and slur markings, and dynamic directions, (3) ability to recognize signature and rhythmic changes several measures ahead of playing, (4) establishment of continuity of thought and sound that results in meaningful performance.

Motivation must be maintained at a high level in class because these skills involve infinite patience, consistent effort, and musical curiosity on the student's part—in fact the small success can and must be so pleasurable that the student will persist until the whole difficult reading process is assimilated and the new skill taken for granted. Good urtext (original) editions should always be used so that when the student learns to read accurately, he reads composers' intentions rather than an editor's suppositions. Rarely does the teacher have to correct a good reader's fingering, because a developed reader has experienced finger patterns that fall into the best position for his hands. Once learned, music-reading can yield life-long pleasure. Moreover, a pause of many years cannot cause the unlearning of this all-important technique.

(1) A good way for hands to establish fingering patterns is to review all major and minor scales and arpeggios and dominant seventh arpeggios in four octaves, hands alone, hands together; scales at intervals of one octave, sixths, tenth; arpeggios in root, first, and second inversion fingering positions: all to be established and maintained daily at six different slow-to-fast metronome speeds.

Each person has a different rate of advancement; sometimes a student can prepare a family of scales and arpeggios in one key in a week, at other times the same accomplishment takes a month. Sometimes an individual can learn and satisfactorily present in this fashion a family of scales and arpeggios on C, D flat, D, in about two weeks for each and then become stumped on the E flat family for no discernible reason other than that the mind learns according to a series of plateaus rather than along a steady uphill curve. Patience, persistence, understanding and, above all, time, are needed to assimilate.

Evenly produced scales and arpeggios are digital skills that anyone can acquire. Care should be given to sound; there should be an ascending crescendo and a descending decrescendo, the legato must melt one note smoothly into the next (not chug-chug in the old-fashioned raised finger method so popular at the turn of the century). Metronome speed should be established at a comfortable level for each student and increased about six steps at each sitting. The ability of individuals in the same class may vary from one note to the beat at each speed, from 80–100 by 4's to two notes to the beat from 120–150 by 6's. (I use an electric or watch metronome and stop between numbers in order to advance evenly at my desired rate.) In all cases the objective is to utilize the scales and arpeggios to establish finger patterns which will be instantly recognized in the initial reading of a composition. There is a great hiatus between *knowing* the scale and *performing* it flawlessly up to tempo in a composition.

(2) There is a great variance in the intermediate student's ability to recognize and perform notes and note-values accurately. So-called "modern" elementary teaching methods fail to stress the necessity to count; "short-cuts," such as relying on a rhythmically patterned accompaniment and repeating parrot-fashion from a teacher's or a recorded performance to establish pulse, are substituted for the actual accounting for every note, dot, and rest on the printed page. I would make all would-be piano teachers perform the rhythmic exercises in Paul Hindemith's book *Fundamentals for the Elementary Musician* before allowing them to become lackadaisical in their teaching to beginners. The student's first solo book should be reinforced by a duet book with counting out loud by the pupil, this to be continued until notes and note-values are a positive, unified concept. It is needlessly discouraging and exceedingly time-consuming to lead a talented student back to the beginning where elemental rhythmic association should be forever established long before multiple accidentals present an added visual hurdle.

At the intermediate level it is possible to guide with material that is attractive, brief, with a minimum of phrase and dynamic markings. Such material should also include elementary ornaments to keep the student aware and unafraid of this new set of symbols while being properly introduced:

Kalmus or Henle edition of Schubert's *Dances*
Peters edition of Corelli's *Pieces for Clavier*

Schott edition of Haydn's *Six Sonatinas*
Padre Soler *Sonatas*
Diabelli *Sonatas and Sonatinas*

None of these are assigned for learning or finishing. Depending on the ability of the student I may ask for only two lines a day hands alone, then hands together, eventually, a whole page every day hands together, later two pages every day hands together. As the student progresses I recommend more difficult material such as:

Kalmus or Schirmer (Kirkpatrick) edition of Scarlatti's *Sonatas*

Paderewski, Henle, or Kalmus edition of Chopin's *Mazurkas* and *Waltzes*

Brahms' *Waltzes*

Henle edition of Schumann *Bunte Blatter* and *Waldescenen*

Tschaikovsky's *Seasons*

Pinto's *Scenas Infantis*

Mignone's *Six Pieces for Children*

These lists present an area where teachers should use imagination; let variety, tone color and style govern choice of material for the individual student. The objective now is to utilize and depend more extensively on phrase and dynamic markings. I ask for one composition every day and at the class meeting I choose one from the assigned group. I don't allow pedaling until the student is quite advanced because this art is too personal and ephemeral; at this stage we want habits that contribute to a strong foundation.

(3) At the same time that students are coordinating fingering patterns on the keyboard with note patterns on the printed page, they should exercise their eyes toward rendering the unexpected. At every class meeting I appoint

two students to look at a duet and play silently at the keyboard while I work on techniques and reading with other students on another piano. The duet players must utilize their optic and tactile senses without help from their ears; they are stimulated by having to read two scores in treble clef or bass clef, one (usually I choose a timid person) has to lead in a melody while the other has to supply a tactful but rhythmic pulse; both are forced to count at the same rate and adjust their rhythm and sound to complement the assigned piece—and they have a limited time to do this *without help from sound!* For this practice I use attractive duets such as:

Mozart's, Schubert's, and Schumann's *Original Music for Four Hands*

Ravel's *Ma Mère l'Oye*

Fauré's *Dolly*

Tschaikovsky's arrangements of Russian Folk Songs; arrangements of Bach's *Brandenburg Concerti*, Bartok's *Short Pieces*, Handel's *Water Music*, etc.

Rachmaninoff's *Italian Polka*

Villa-Lobos' *Little Train of the Caipira*

After their short silent practice period my performing duo get a real sense of accomplishment when they read for us their new instant production.

To make my solo readers develop their eyes' comprehension I will assign to strengthen phrase and touch skills:

Bartok's *For Children* (both volumes)

Prokofieff's *Visions Fugitives*

Shostakovich, Scriabin, and Ginastera *Preludes*

La Montaine's *Child's Picture Book Suite*

Ravel's *Valses Nobles et Sentimentales*

Barber's *Excursions*

The objective is to strengthen dependence on eyes as well as on ears for reading accidentals and unexpected rhythmic combinations.

(4) To establish continuity through the sight-reading procedure, metronome pulse should be established somewhat slower, below reading ability. Really good music sounds fine at a variety of tempi; a slow musical reading of a Bach Prelude is infinitely preferable to a hurried, slapdash, stuttered rendition that cannot be listened to by the performer because he is too busy. A triple translation takes place: (a) the mind assimilates the directions on the printed page, (b) the fingers have to accomplish these tasks, and (c) the ears and mind have to monitor and adjust the results. Such coordination takes time; slow metronome practice can establish the necessary pulse while the coordination span is stretched, brought under control. Over a period of time the metronome's speed is gently raised until a pulse approaching the right tempo can be established, even at a first attempt.

Class work has the advantages of reducing a performer's self-consciousness to a minimum and of motivating concentration to a maximum. Mistakes assume their true unimportance and music-making becomes a game where there are only winners who enjoy all the attending triumphs. The tape-recorder testifies that two ninety-minute meetings a week plus a daily half-hour at home will bring dramatic results to five class students in a semester.

Truly effective music readers always progress. They play chamber music, accompany, explore solo repertoire, experiment with their personal musical contributions. A developed reader is a disciplined, useful musician who is free to look ahead with pride to the unfolding of his own musical personality.

16

FROM STUDIO TO STAGE

AHEAD, ALMOST within reach, is *your* mental concept of a given musical composition. *Now* is the time to carry it out of the studio — to try staging it.

A composition is ready for its first venture as soon as it is thoroughly pre-learned and memorized, especially if the memorization is the result of careful practice rather than speedily forced. Sooner is better than later; if you wait until a composition is "ready" before playing, it will never reach that state even if it is steadily worked over a long period.

Go to the piano at a non-practice time, put down the music rack, raise the lid of the grand, and plunge as if you were in Carnegie Hall. Find out how much control you have under unrehearsed conditions. It may take five or six consecutive performances that first session before you get *one* that holds together well enough to make musical sense. The first time you will be too busy playing to listen while you play. Technical weakness, vague phrasing, unwieldy fingering, clumsy pedaling rise to the surface; you learn what and where to correct. The music unfolds new moods that you never dreamed were there. Fresh ideas should be immediately compared with the score so that the imagination becomes disciplined by the composer's expressed directions. Try something unusual such as a much higher or much lower seat, or play with one eye shut, or change the position of the piano to face another direction—anything to alter the usual aspect of the room so that habits of awareness are upset and listening is intensified. There should be experimentation with tempo and dynamic detail until your music sounds almost the way you want it. After several such rehearsals, supplemented by regular practice, the composition will succeed in *one* spontaneous performance.

Then play on another piano and find an indulgent listener. Again your musical concept will undergo changes as conditioned by the new piano, or as you listen with the empathy of another person. It will take several such sallies, in addition to routine practice, to make the new composition moderately controllable. The more often you play, the more flexible your performance will become.

Work for beautiful sound. Even if the musical concept is too unexplored to be convincing, a good sound will be inviting. Push with body weight to get the richest sound in the instrument. Review the score for permanent dynamic markings such as pp, p, mp, mf, f, and ff. Make all other markings such as accents, fz, sf, diminuendo and crescendo fit into the larger tonal framework. Look for crescendos that need to be guided on a downward melodic line, and for diminuendos that fade away on a rising melody. Avoid unnecessary accents. Play groups of chords melodically, listening for horizontal rather than vertical line. Raise your hands wrists up and release your melody line last so that the sound lingers. Explore inner voices and emphasize their harmonic and melodic contribution. Experiment with timbre and different textures of legato, staccato, and pedal to create mood; the piano can recreate the effect of an orchestra. Separate the combinations of diminuendo and ritardando, crescendo and accelerando. Use the metronome to monitor all passages marked with ritardando, rallentando, and sostenuto. Literally play by ear; use special methods on each instrument until you succeed musically under all circumstances.

Make your musical lines as long as possible. Rachmaninoff said, "Small musician, small ideas; big musician, big ideas." After an artist has played a program many times he can soar so high above the music that he conceives the whole event in one arch of sound. Make each phrase prepare for the next; make many phrases into a single strong musical line. When the composer permits, make your phrase endings point upward until you have finished your musical paragraph. Hold audience attention by making the peak of your musical arch near the end of the idea. Try inverted arches; for variety combine several arches so that they form a dynamic circle. Play legato with fingers; here the pedal should supplement rather than cause liquid sound. Obey the composer's written phrase slurs; make a difference between the small raise-wrist sound of small phrase groupings and the arm-guided ending of a final cadence. Phrasing should be as natural as speaking, never predictably the same, but expressive of innuendo as well as thought.

Establish "stations" at various places in a new composition as guide-posts for emergency use. It should be possible to start from any one of these "stations." In polyphonic compositions proceed from station to station in both forward and reverse order: for example, if there are eight stations in a composition, it is extra insurance for the performer to be able to start at 1, 2, 3, 4, 5, 6, 7, 8, or 8, 7, 6, 5, 4, 3, 2, or 1.

Additional metronome practice should be given to stubborn spots as a supplement to practicing a composition from beginning to end. A weak passage can poison a performance by slowing the mental flow from ideas to notes, and thereby cause a breakdown in an innocuous non-problem place. Practice the difficult passage at six metronome speeds below that at which you start to practice the entire piece. For instance, if you practice the entire composition from 80-100 by 4's, prepare the troublesome spot by practicing from 70-80 by 2's.

This is comparable to putting an extra pad of carpet over a traffic area in order to keep the whole carpet intact.

Cultivate the habit of technical perfection. Daily maintenance is essential to every composition for the length of time that you wish to keep it available for performance. I consider a daily minimum to be six technically correct performances at evenly measured metronome speeds from too slow, through the correct tempo, to too fast. For instance 80-100 by 4's if you wish to play at about 92, or 100-130 by 6's if you wish to play at about 120. This daily routine applies to a nocturne as well as to an etude. Somehow the same amount of work takes literally four or five times longer when a composition is new than when it is comfortably seasoned. I like to think of this as the post-learning process. It is a most exciting learning experience because the technical problems are understood, communication becomes possible, and new evaluations prompt bolder experiments with touch and phrasing.

Early performances should be at a more deliberate tempo than the top practiced speed. Experienced artists know how to depend on beautiful sound to maintain interest while they play slowly in an early public performance so that there can be as much relaxation under stress as possible. Perform slowly until experience gives greater freedom.

Give your, musical feeling at all times. Musical detail is "built-in" by slow metronome practice. It should not be possible to turn musicality on and off like a light switch, yet many students practice in a dry mechanical manner and have to be persuaded, extolled, literally pulled into the proper mood before they reveal their true musical feelings. It is not enough for the performer to "feel"; he has to project those feelings to the audience. This is the communicator's art, and demands more practice than any technical problem. Artists do not wait to be in a mood in order to communicate; they create mood for their audience by communicating.

A composition is yours only when it is thoroughly in your subconscious. A famous violin teacher has his students play standing on one foot with the other held straight out in front; the students have to concentrate so hard on maintaining their balance that they depend on their subconscious to play. Invite a friend to maintain a running conversation with you while you rehearse. The more you can consign to your subconscious, the freer you are to make music.

It is possible to pre-learn and finish learning a composition, and still have it so clumsy that you are too wary of it to persist through the post-learning maintenance. When this happens, if the piece is completely memorized and you've actually performed it enough times to know that it can enjoy life in your repertoire, put it away for seasoning until some later time when you can re-learn it. However don't give up too soon. Most people do. You can induce a shortened artificial seasoning period by learning several small compositions such as the different movements of a suite in this way:

Learn number one until it is memorized.

Learn number two until it is memorized.

Learn number three until it is memorized.

Learn number four and review number one at the same time. Number one will come back better than it was. Play it on several occasions. Continue learning number four until memorized.

After you perform number one successfully and comfortably, drop number one and review number two until it is completely finished.

When number four is memorized, proceed to learn number five.

Proceed in this way learning one piece while finishing another piece until the whole suite is conquered, and each part performed.

Use this method with a sonata, a whole book of preludes

or etudes, or in assembling a whole program. You can divide an enormously difficult composition into small parts and learn each part as described above. Most "difficult" pieces are simply too much to assimilate all at once. After each small section is learned there will be several musical and mental adjustments as you develop a concept of the complete work.

To correct persistent memory blanks a supplemental review with the open score both at the piano and away from the instrument is helpful. Analyze the harmonic scheme and make a melody of intervals, or make a chord of a melody line. Sometimes the eyes or ears will catch a musical idea that all the muscle reflexes have failed to assimilate. The open score should always be available during practice periods to indicate the composer's wishes.

Every artist becomes bored during certain stages of learning. Slow metronome practice invariably makes one yawn; thousands of extraneous details float into the mind: important phone calls, laundry lists, minor aches and pains. Rachmaninoff wrote that sitting to complete a practice assignment is part of musical talent. Try setting a plain kitchen timer for twenty minutes; see how much you can accomplish on a specific passage before the timer bell rings. Alternate practice methods in order to save time; one day work only with shifting accents, the next day use a combination of accents with controlled dynamics, the following day metronome with accents, then metronome with controlled dynamics. Use many approaches to "out-sit" the problem. Have patience with yourself! It is always more beneficial to work for a limited time every day than to cram for a long period on isolated days.

When preparing a program make a habit of playing the opening number every time you sit down at a piano—at home or visiting, for an audience or for yourself. That composition should be almost automatically perfect because the unaccustomed atmosphere of lights, stage, audience cause unforseen self-consciousness. When possible, practice on the concert piano at the hall both the day before and the day of the concert; overnight concentration on problems concerning the handling of the instrument makes them disappear. The more you practice on the instrument, the better the concert. Work out an attractive lighting system for the stage; the public will enjoy what they hear more if they like what they see. I like as much pink light as I can get on stage, and a dark auditorium. Get a friend to sit in front of the piano, and experiment with the available lights until you find a combination you like.

On the morning of the concert give at least six metronome speeds to everything you intend to play; take nothing for granted and have the satisfaction of knowing that you did what you could to play well. Give a double round of metronome and accents to all problem spots. Stop all metronome work at two speeds below your normal top practice speed.

Eat lightly before the concert; scrambled eggs or cottage cheese will fill you without bloating. Avoid coffee; sometimes caffeine can make your hands shake. (If your heels or knees do shake in concert, simply take your feet off the pedals; it is better to err on the side of clarity than to let a heavy foot spoil a performance.) Take a half-hour rest flat on your back two hours before concert time. Dress and go back to work on your silent keyboard with music and metronome back stage. Work on rough passages only. Start with your last encore, and proceed through the whole program in reverse order so that the last number which you review will be the first number you play on stage. While the stage lights are being adjusted do a few quick up-down touch-the-ceiling touch-the-floor calisthenics to get the blood circulating. When the auditorium lights are out, wait for the audience to hush. You will feel the rosy glow in your cheeks and in your fingertips. Look as if you're glad to see your audience; if you are steadfast it may be your privilege to create a memorable event.

A postlude in the name of truth: there is no such thing as a flawless performance. Have faith in your ultimate success especially after failures; know that consistent effort will bring increasingly good results. Paderewski's statement that "Stage-fright is bad musical conscience" is partially misunderstood; people confuse "fright" with "excitement." The great artists all experience tremendous stage excitement; creativity is an awe-inspiring responsibility. During early performances there will be many rough passages as your studio preparation and your musical concept seem to battle for supremacy. If, during the excitement of performance, you have an inspiration to try a new interpretation, go along with it even if contrary to all your previous training. Check afterwards with the score in order to know whether you have come up with an idea to add permanently. When you forget the baser problems of technique, you will begin to make music which is freed by creative experience. You must give completely of yourself; the few moments of creative satisfaction that are your reward are magical.